HBR Guide to
Being
a Great Boss

Harvard Business Review Guides

Arm yourself with the advice you need to succeed on the job, from the most trusted brand in business. Packed with how-to essentials from leading experts, the HBR Guides provide smart answers to your most pressing work challenges.

The titles include:

HBR Guide for Women at Work

HBR Guide to Being a Great Boss

HBR Guide to Being More Productive

HBR Guide to Better Business Writing

HBR Guide to Building Your Business Case

HBR Guide to Buying a Small Business

HBR Guide to Changing Your Career

HBR Guide to Coaching Employees

HBR Guide to Collaborative Teams

HBR Guide to Data Analytics Basics for Managers

HBR Guide to Dealing with Conflict

HBR Guide to Delivering Effective Feedback

HBR Guide to Emotional Intelligence

HBR Guide to Finance Basics for Managers

HBR Guide to Getting the Mentoring You Need

HBR Guide to Getting the Right Job

HBR Guide to Getting the Right Work Done

HBR Guide to Leading Teams

HBR Guide to Making Better Decisions

HBR Guide to
Being a Great Boss

HARVARD BUSINESS REVIEW PRESS

Boston, Massachusetts

The web addresses referenced in this book were live and correct at the time of the book's publication but may be subject to change.

Cataloging-in-Publication data is forthcoming.

ISBN: 978-1-64782-234-7
eISBN: 978-1-64782-235-4

The paper used in this publication meets the requirements of the American National Standard for Permanence of Paper for Publications and Documents in Libraries and Archives Z39.48-1992.

What You'll Learn

No one has a more significant impact on your employees' day-to-day experience than you, their manager. A great boss—someone who is supportive, helpful, proactive, and thoughtful—is a joy to work for. A bad one . . . well, as the saying goes, people don't leave companies because of their jobs.

But what separates so-so managers from next-level bosses? Maybe you know how to read a P&L, set and implement strategy, and hire new team members. But do you know how to develop trusting relationships with your employees? Can you create a culture where failing is an opportunity to learn? Does your feedback give employees a clear path toward their goals? Are you the kind of boss people *want* to work for?

Whether you are new to managing or have been leading a team for years, this guide will help you go beyond the basics so that you can help every employee thrive.

You'll learn how to:

- Motivate and engage your team

- Build a culture of trust and psychological safety

- Meet the needs of both B players and stars

- Support employees struggling with mental health issues

- Share—and receive—useful feedback

- Help people find purpose in their work

- Ensure employees from all backgrounds feel welcome

- Keep in-office and remote workers connected and productive

- Get underperformers back on track

- Be authentically yourself

Contents

Contents

SECTION THREE

Give Feedback and Motivate

SECTION FOUR

Manage Everyone Effectively

Contents

What Being a Great Boss Means

CHAPTER 1

What Great Managers Do

by Marcus Buckingham

"The best boss I ever had." That's a phrase most of us have said or heard at some point, but what does it mean? What sets the great boss apart from the average boss? The literature is rife with provocative writing about the qualities of managers and leaders and whether the two differ, but little has been said about what happens in the thousands of daily interactions and decisions that allows managers to get the best out of their people and win their devotion. What do great managers actually *do*?

In my research, beginning with a survey of 80,000 managers conducted by the Gallup Organization and

Excerpted from an article in *Harvard Business Review*, March 2005 (product #R0503D).

continuing during the past two years with in-depth studies of a few top performers, I've found that while there are as many styles of management as there are managers, there is one quality that sets truly great managers apart from the rest: They discover what is unique about each person and then capitalize on it. Average managers play checkers, while great managers play chess. The difference? In checkers, all the pieces are uniform and move in the same way; they are interchangeable. You need to plan and coordinate their movements, certainly, but they all move at the same pace, on parallel paths. In chess, each type of piece moves in a different way, and you can't play if you don't know how each piece moves. More important, you won't win if you don't think carefully about how you move the pieces. Great managers know and value the unique abilities and even the eccentricities of their employees, and they learn how best to integrate them into a coordinated plan of attack.

This is the exact opposite of what great leaders do. Great leaders discover what is universal and capitalize on it. Their job is to rally people toward a better future. Leaders can succeed in this only when they can cut through differences of race, sex, age, nationality, and personality and, using stories and celebrating heroes, tap into those very few needs we all share. The job of a manager, meanwhile, is to turn one person's particular talent into performance. Managers will succeed only when they can identify and deploy the differences among people, challenging each employee to excel in his or her own way. This doesn't mean a leader can't be a manager or vice versa. But to excel at one or both, you must be aware of the very different skills each role requires. (See the sidebar "The Elusive 'One Thing.'")

The Game of Chess

What does the chess game look like in action? When I visited Michelle Miller, the manager who opened Walgreens' 4,000th store, I found the wall of her back office papered with work schedules. Michelle's store in Redondo Beach, California, employs people with sharply different skills and potentially disruptive differences in personality. A critical part of her job, therefore, is to put people into roles and shifts that will allow them to shine—and to avoid putting clashing personalities together. At the same time, she needs to find ways for individuals to grow.

There's Jeffrey, for example, a "goth rocker" whose hair is shaved on one side and long enough on the other side to cover his face. Michelle almost didn't hire him because he couldn't quite look her in the eye during his interview, but he wanted the hard-to-cover night shift, so she decided to give him a chance. After a couple of months, she noticed that when she gave Jeffrey a vague assignment, such as "Straighten up the merchandise in every aisle," what should have been a two-hour job would take him all night—and wouldn't be done very well. But if she gave him a more specific task, such as "Put up all the risers for Christmas," all the risers would be symmetrical, with the right merchandise on each one, perfectly priced, labeled, and "faced" (turned toward the customer). Give Jeffrey a generic task, and he would struggle. Give him one that forced him to be accurate and analytical, and he would excel. This, Michelle concluded, was Jeffrey's

5

THE ELUSIVE "ONE THING"

It's bold to characterize anything as *the* explanation or solution, so it's a risky move to make such definitive assertions as "this is the one thing all great managers do." But with enough research and focus, it is possible to identify that elusive "one thing."

I like to think of the concept of "one thing" as a "controlling insight." Controlling insights don't explain all outcomes or events; they serve as the best explanation of the greatest number of events. Such insights help you know which of your actions will have the most far-reaching influence in virtually every situation.

For a concept to emerge as the single controlling insight, it must pass three tests. First, it must be applicable across a wide range of situations. Take leadership as an example. Lately, much has been made of the notion that there is no one best way to lead and that instead, the most effective leadership style depends on the circumstance. While there is no doubt that different situations require different actions from a leader, that doesn't mean the most insightful thing you can say about leadership is that it's situational. With

forte. So, as any good manager would do, she told him what she had deduced about him and praised him for his good work.

And a good manager would have left it at that. But Michelle knew she could get more out of Jeffrey. So she devised a scheme to reassign responsibilities across the entire store to capitalize on his unique strengths. In enough focus, you can identify the one thing that underpins successful leadership across all situations and all styles.

Second, a controlling insight must serve as a multiplier. In any equation, some factors will have only an additive value: When you focus your actions on these factors, you see some incremental improvement. The controlling insight should be more powerful. It should show you how to get exponential improvement. For example, good managing is the result of a combination of many actions—selecting talented employees, setting clear expectations, catching people doing things right, and so on—but none of these factors qualifies as the "one thing" that great managers do, because even when done well, these actions merely prevent managers from chasing their best employees away.

Finally, the controlling insight must guide action. It must point to precise things that can be done to create better outcomes more consistently. Insights that managers can act on—rather than simply ruminate over—are the ones that can make all the difference.

every Walgreens, there is a responsibility called "resets and revisions." A reset involves stocking an aisle with new merchandise, a task that usually coincides with a predictable change in customer buying patterns (at the end of summer, for example, the stores will replace sun creams and lip balms with allergy medicines). A revision is a less time-consuming but more frequent version of the same thing: Replace these cartons of toothpaste with this new and improved variety. Display this new line of detergent at this end of the row. Each aisle requires some form of revision at least once a week.

In most Walgreens stores, each employee "owns" one aisle, where she is responsible not only for serving customers but also for facing the merchandise, keeping the aisle clean and orderly, tagging items with a Telxon gun, and conducting all resets and revisions. This arrangement is simple and efficient, and it affords each employee a sense of personal responsibility. But Michelle decided that since Jeffrey was so good at resets and revisions—and didn't enjoy interacting with customers—this should be his full-time job, in every single aisle.

It was a challenge. One week's worth of revisions requires a binder three inches thick. But Michelle reasoned that not only would Jeffrey be excited by the challenge and get better and better with practice, but other employees would be freed from what they considered a chore and have more time to greet and serve customers. The store's performance proved her right. After the reorganization, Michelle saw not only increases in sales and profit but also in that most critical performance metric, customer satisfaction. In the subsequent four months, her store netted perfect scores in Walgreens' mystery shopper program.

So far, so very good. Sadly, it didn't last. This "perfect" arrangement depended on Jeffrey remaining content, and he didn't. With his success at doing resets and revisions, his confidence grew, and six months into the job, he wanted to move into management. Michelle wasn't disappointed by this, however; she was intrigued. She had watched Jeffrey's progress closely and had already decided that he might do well as a manager, though he wouldn't be a particularly emotive one. Besides, like any good chess player, she had been thinking a couple of moves ahead.

Over in the cosmetics aisle worked an employee named Genoa. Michelle saw Genoa as something of a double threat. Not only was she adept at putting customers at ease—she remembered their names, asked good questions, was welcoming yet professional when answering the phone—but she was also a neatnik. The cosmetics department was always perfectly faced, every product remained aligned, and everything was arranged just so. Her aisle was sexy: It made you want to reach out and touch the merchandise.

To capitalize on these twin talents, and to accommodate Jeffrey's desire for promotion, Michelle shuffled the roles within the store once again. She split Jeffrey's reset and revision job in two and gave the "revision" part of it to Genoa so that the whole store could now benefit from her ability to arrange merchandise attractively. But Michelle didn't want the store to miss out on Genoa's gift for customer service, so Michelle asked her to focus on the revision role only between 8:30 a.m. and 11:30 a.m., and after that, when the store began to fill with customers on their lunch breaks, Genoa should shift her focus over to them.

She kept the reset role with Jeffrey. Assistant managers don't usually have an ongoing responsibility in the store, but, Michelle reasoned, he was now so good and so fast at tearing an aisle apart and rebuilding it that he could easily finish a major reset during a five-hour stint, so he could handle resets along with his managerial responsibilities.

By the time you read this, the Jeffrey–Genoa configuration has probably outlived its usefulness, and Michelle has moved on to design other effective and inventive configurations. The ability to keep tweaking roles to capitalize on the uniqueness of each person is the essence of great management.

A manager's approach to capitalizing on differences can vary tremendously from place to place. Walk into the back office at another Walgreens, this one in San Jose, California, managed by Jim Kawashima, and you won't see a single work schedule. Instead, the walls are covered with sales figures and statistics, the best of them circled with red felt-tip pen, and dozens of photographs of sales contest winners, most featuring a customer service representative named Manjit.

Manjit outperforms her peers consistently. When I first heard about her, she had just won a competition in Walgreens' suggestive selling program to sell the most units of Gillette deodorant in a month. The national average was 300; Manjit had sold 1,600. Disposable cameras, toothpaste, batteries—you name it, she could sell it. And Manjit won contest after contest despite working the graveyard shift, from 12:30 a.m. to 8:30 a.m., during which she met significantly fewer customers than did her peers.

Manjit hadn't always been such an exceptional performer. She became stunningly successful only when Jim, who has made a habit of resuscitating troubled stores, came on board. What did Jim do to initiate the change in Manjit? He quickly picked up on her idiosyncrasies and figured out how to translate them into outstanding performance. For example, back in India, Manjit was an athlete—a runner and a weight lifter—and had always thrilled to the challenge of measured performance. When I interviewed her, one of the first things out of her mouth was, "On Saturday, I sold 343 low-carb candy bars. On Sunday, I sold 367. Yesterday, 110, and today, 105." I asked if she always knows how well she's doing. "Oh yes," she replied. "Every day I check Mr. K's charts. Even on my day off, I make a point to come in and check my numbers."

Manjit loves to win and revels in public recognition. Hence, Jim's walls are covered with charts and figures, Manjit's scores are always highlighted in red, and there are photos documenting her success. Another manager might have asked Manjit to curb her enthusiasm for the limelight and give someone else a chance. Jim found a way to capitalize on it.

But what about Jim's other staff members? Instead of being resentful of Manjit's public recognition, the other employees came to understand that Jim took the time to see them as individuals and evaluate them based on their personal strengths. They also knew that Manjit's success spoke well of the entire store, so her success galvanized the team. In fact, before long, the pictures of Manjit began to include other employees from the store, too. After a few months, the San Jose location was ranked number one out of 4,000 in Walgreens' suggestive selling program.

Great Managers Are Romantics

Think back to Michelle. Her creative choreography may sound like a last resort, an attempt to make the best of a bad hire. It's not. Jeffrey and Genoa are not mediocre employees, and capitalizing on each person's uniqueness is a tremendously powerful tool.

First, identifying and capitalizing on each person's uniqueness saves time. No employee, however talented, is perfectly well-rounded. Michelle could have spent untold hours coaching Jeffrey and cajoling him into smiling at, making friends with, and remembering the names of customers, but she probably would have seen little result for her efforts. Her time was much better spent carving out a role that took advantage of Jeffrey's natural abilities.

Second, capitalizing on uniqueness makes each person more accountable. Michelle didn't just praise Jeffrey for his ability to execute specific assignments. She challenged him to make this ability the cornerstone of his contribution to the store, to take ownership for this ability, to practice it, and to refine it.

Third, capitalizing on what is unique about each person builds a stronger sense of team, because it creates interdependency. It helps people appreciate one another's particular skills and learn that their coworkers can fill in where they are lacking. In short, it makes people need one another. The old cliché is that there's no "I" in "team." But as Michael Jordan once said, "There may be no 'I' in 'team,' but there is in 'win.'"

Finally, when you capitalize on what is unique about each person, you introduce a healthy degree of disruption into your world. You shuffle existing hierarchies: If Jeffrey is in charge of all resets and revisions in the store, should he now command more or less respect than an assistant manager? You also shuffle existing assumptions about who is allowed to do what: If Jeffrey devises new methods of resetting an aisle, does he have to ask permission to try these out, or can he experiment on his own? And you shuffle existing beliefs about where the true expertise lies: If Genoa comes up with a way of arranging new merchandise that she thinks is more appealing than the method suggested by the "planogram" sent down from Walgreens headquarters, does her expertise trump the planners back at corporate? These questions will challenge Walgreens' orthodoxies and thus will help the company become more inquisitive, more intelligent, more vital, and, despite its size, more able to duck and weave into the future.

All that said, the reason great managers focus on uniqueness isn't just because it makes good business sense. They do it because they can't help it. Like Shelley and Keats, the 19th-century Romantic poets, great managers are fascinated with individuality for its own sake. Fine shadings of personality, though they may be invisible to some and frustrating to others, are crystal clear to and highly valued by great managers. They could no more ignore these subtleties than ignore their own needs and desires. Figuring out what makes people tick is simply in their nature.

The Three Levers

Although the Romantics were mesmerized by differences, at some point, managers need to rein in their inquisitiveness, gather up what they know about a person, and put the employee's idiosyncrasies to use. To that end, there are three things you must know about someone to manage her well: her strengths, the triggers that activate those strengths, and how she learns.

Make the most of strengths

It takes time and effort to gain a full appreciation of an employee's strengths and weaknesses. The great manager spends a good deal of time outside the office walking around, watching each person's reactions to events, listening, and taking mental notes about what each individual is drawn to and what each person struggles with. There's no substitute for this kind of observation, but you can obtain a lot of information about a person by asking a few simple, open-ended questions and listening carefully to the answers. Two queries in particular have proven most revealing when it comes to identifying strengths and weaknesses, and I recommend

---

What you need to know about each of your direct reports

- ☐ What are his or her strengths?
- ☐ What are the triggers that activate those strengths?
- ☐ What is his or her learning style?

---

asking them of all new hires—and revisiting the questions periodically.

To identify a person's strengths, first ask, "What was the best day at work you've had in the past three months?" Find out what the person was doing and why he enjoyed it so much. Remember: A strength is not merely something you are good at. In fact, it might be something you aren't good at yet. It might be just a predilection, something you find so intrinsically satisfying that you look forward to doing it again and again and getting better at it over time. This question will prompt your employee to start thinking about his interests and abilities from this perspective.

To identify a person's weaknesses, just invert the question: "What was the worst day you've had at work in the past three months?" And then probe for details about what he was doing and why it grated on him so much. As with a strength, a weakness is not merely something you are bad at (in fact, you might be quite competent at it). It is something that drains you of energy, an activity that you never look forward to doing and that when you are doing it, all you can think about is stopping.

Although you're keeping an eye out for both the strengths and weaknesses of your employees, your focus should be on their strengths. Conventional wisdom holds that self-awareness is a good thing and that it's the job of the manager to identify weaknesses and create a plan for overcoming them. But research by Albert Bandura, the father of social learning theory, has shown that self-assurance (labeled "self-efficacy" by cognitive psychologists), not self-awareness, is the strongest predictor of a person's ability to set high goals, to persist in the face of obstacles, to bounce back when reversals occur, and, ultimately, to achieve the goals they set. By contrast, self-awareness has not been shown to be a predictor of any of these outcomes, and in some cases, it appears to retard them.

Great managers seem to understand this instinctively. They know that their job is not to arm each employee with a dispassionately accurate understanding of the limits of her strengths and the liabilities of her weaknesses but to reinforce her self-assurance. That's why great managers focus on strengths. When a person succeeds, the great manager doesn't praise her hard work. Even if there's some exaggeration in the statement, he tells her that she succeeded because she has become so good at deploying her specific strengths. This, the manager knows, will strengthen the employee's self-assurance and make her more optimistic and more resilient in the face of challenges to come.

The focus-on-strengths approach might create in the employee a modicum of overconfidence, but great managers mitigate this by emphasizing the size and the difficulty of the employee's goals. They know that their primary objective is to create in each employee a specific state of mind: one that includes a realistic assessment of the difficulty of the obstacle ahead but an unrealistically optimistic belief in her ability to overcome it.

And what if the employee fails? Assuming the failure is not attributable to factors beyond her control, always explain failure as a lack of effort, even if this is only partially accurate. This will obscure self-doubt and give her something to work on as she faces up to the next challenge.

Repeated failure, of course, may indicate weakness where a role requires strength. In such cases, there are four approaches for overcoming weaknesses. If the problem amounts to a lack of skill or knowledge, that's easy to solve: Simply offer the relevant training, allow some time for the employee to incorporate the new skills, and look for signs of improvement. If her performance doesn't get better, you'll know that the reason she's struggling is because she is missing certain talents, a deficit no amount of skill or knowledge training is likely to fix. You'll have to find a way to manage around this weakness and neutralize it.

Which brings us to the second strategy for overcoming an employee weakness. Can you find her a partner, someone whose talents are strong in precisely the areas where hers are weak? Here's how this strategy can look in action. As vice president of merchandising for the women's clothing retailer Ann Taylor, Judi Langley found that tensions were rising between her and one of her merchandising managers, Claudia (not her real name), whose analytical mind and intense nature created an overpowering "need to know." If Claudia learned of something before Judi had a chance to review it with her, she would become deeply frustrated. Given the speed with which decisions were made, and given Judi's busy schedule, this happened frequently. Judi was concerned that Claudia's irritation was unsettling the whole product team, not to mention earning the employee a reputation as a malcontent.

An average manager might have identified this behavior as a weakness and lectured Claudia on how to control her need for information. Judi, however, realized that this "weakness" was an aspect of Claudia's greatest strength: her analytical mind. Claudia would never be able to rein it in, at least not for long. So Judi looked for a strategy that would honor and support Claudia's need to know, while channeling it more productively. Judi decided to act as Claudia's information partner, and she committed to leaving Claudia a voice mail at the end of each day with a brief update. To make sure nothing fell through the cracks, they set up two live "touch base" conversations per week. This solution managed Claudia's expectations and assured her that she would get the information she needed, if not exactly when she wanted it, then at least at frequent and predictable intervals. Giving Claudia a partner neutralized the negative manifestations of her strength, allowing her to focus her analytical mind on her work. (Of course, in most cases, the partner would need to be someone other than a manager.)

Should the perfect partner prove hard to find, try this third strategy: Insert into the employee's world a technique that helps accomplish through discipline what the person can't accomplish through instinct. I met one very successful screenwriter and director who had struggled with telling other professionals, such as composers and directors of photography, that their work was not up to snuff. So he devised a mental trick: He now imagines what the "god of art" would want and uses this imaginary entity as a source of strength. In his mind, he no longer imposes his own opinion on his colleagues but rather tells himself (and them) that an authoritative third party has weighed in.

If training produces no improvement, if complementary partnering proves impractical, and if no nifty discipline technique can be found, you are going to have to try the fourth and final strategy, which is to rearrange the employee's working world to render his weakness irrelevant, as Michelle Miller did with Jeffrey. This strategy will require of you, first, the creativity to envision a more effective arrangement and, second, the courage to make that arrangement work. But as Michelle's experience revealed, the payoff that may come in the form of increased employee productivity and engagement is well worth it.

Trigger good performance

A person's strengths aren't always on display. Sometimes they require precise triggering to turn them on. Squeeze the right trigger, and a person will push himself harder and persevere in the face of resistance. Squeeze the wrong one, and the person may well shut down. This can be tricky because triggers come in myriad and mysterious forms. One employee's trigger might be tied to the time of day (he is a night owl, and his strengths only kick in after 3 p.m.). Another employee's trigger might be tied to time with you, the boss (even though he's worked with you for more than five years, he still needs you to check in with him every day, or he feels he's being ignored).

Another worker's trigger might be just the opposite—independence (she's only worked for you for six months, but if you check in with her even once a week, she feels micromanaged).

The most powerful trigger by far is recognition, not money. If you're not convinced of this, start ignoring one of your highly paid stars, and watch what happens. Most managers are aware that employees respond well to recognition. Great managers refine and extend this insight. They realize that each employee plays to a slightly different audience. To excel as a manager, you must be able to match the employee to the audience he values most. One employee's audience might be his peers; the best way to praise him would be to stand him up in front of his coworkers and publicly celebrate his achievement. Another's favorite audience might be you; the most powerful recognition would be a one-on-one conversation where you tell him quietly but vividly why he is such a valuable member of the team. Still another employee might define himself by his expertise; his most prized form of recognition would be some type of professional or technical award. Yet another might value feedback only from customers, in which case a picture of the employee with her best customer or a letter to her from the customer would be the best form of recognition.

Given how much personal attention it requires, tailoring praise to fit the person is mostly a manager's responsibility. But organizations can take a cue from this, too. There's no reason why a large company can't take this individualized approach to recognition and apply it to every employee. Of all the companies I've encountered, the North American division of HSBC, a London-based bank, has done the best job of this. Each year it presents its top individual consumer-lending performers with its Dream Awards. Each winner receives a unique prize. During the year, managers ask employees to identify what they would like to receive should they win. The prize value is capped at $10,000, and it cannot be redeemed as cash, but beyond those two restrictions, each employee is free to pick the prize he wants. At the end of the year, the company holds a Dream Awards gala, during which it shows a video about the winning employee and why he selected his particular prize.

You can imagine the impact these personalized prizes have on HSBC employees. It's one thing to be brought up on stage and given yet another plaque. It's another thing when, in addition to public recognition of your performance, you receive a college tuition fund for your child, or the Harley-Davidson motorcycle you've always dreamed of, or—the prize everyone at the company still talks about—the airline tickets to fly you and your family back to Mexico to visit the grandmother you haven't seen in 10 years.

Tailor to learning styles

Although there are many learning styles, a careful review of adult learning theory reveals that three styles predominate. These three are not mutually exclusive; certain employees may rely on a combination of two or perhaps all three. Nonetheless, staying attuned to each employee's style or styles will help focus your coaching.

First, there's analyzing. Claudia from Ann Taylor is an analyzer. She understands a task by taking it apart, examining its elements, and reconstructing it piece by piece. Because every single component of a task is important in her eyes, she craves information. She needs to absorb all there is to know about a subject before she can begin to feel comfortable with it. If she doesn't feel she has enough information, she will dig and push until she gets it. She will read the assigned reading. She will attend the required classes. She will take good notes. She will study. And she will still want more.

The best way to teach an analyzer is to give her ample time in the classroom. Role-play with her. Do postmortem exercises with her. Break her performance down into its component parts so she can carefully build it back up. Always allow her time to prepare. The analyzer hates mistakes. A commonly held view is that mistakes fuel learning, but for the analyzer, this just isn't true. In fact, the reason she prepares so diligently is to minimize the possibility of mistakes. So don't expect to teach her much by throwing her into a new situation and telling her to wing it.

The opposite is true for the second dominant learning style, doing. While the most powerful learning moments for the analyzer occur prior to the performance, the doer's most powerful moments occur *during* the performance. Trial and error are integral to this learning process. Jeffrey, from Michelle Miller's store, is a doer. He learns the most while he's in the act of figuring things out for himself. For him, preparation is a dry, uninspiring activity. So rather than role-play with someone like Jeffrey, pick a specific task within his role that is simple but real, give him a brief overview of the outcomes you want, and get out of his way. Then gradually increase the degree of each task's complexity until he has mastered every aspect of his role. He may make a few mistakes along the way, but for the doer, mistakes are the raw material for learning.

Finally, there's watching. Watchers won't learn much through role-playing. They won't learn by doing, either. Since most formal training programs incorporate both of these elements, watchers are often viewed as rather poor students. That may be true, but they aren't necessarily poor learners.

Watchers can learn a great deal when they are given the chance to see the total performance. Studying the individual parts of a task is about as meaningful for them as studying the individual pixels of a digital photograph. What's important for this type of learner is the content of each pixel, its position relative to all the others. Watchers are only able to see this when they view the complete picture.

As it happens, this is the way I learn. Years ago, when I first began interviewing, I struggled to learn the skill of creating a report on a person after I had interviewed him. I understood all the required steps, but I couldn't seem to put them together. Some of my colleagues could knock out a report in an hour; for me, it would take the better part of a day. Then one afternoon, as I was staring morosely into my Dictaphone, I overheard the voice of the analyst next door. He was talking so rapidly that I initially thought he was on the phone. Only after a few minutes did I realize that he was dictating a report. This was the first time I had heard someone "in the act." I'd seen the finished results countless times, since reading the reports of others was the way we were supposed to learn, but I'd never actually heard another analyst in the act of creation. It was a revelation. I finally saw how everything should come together into a coherent whole. I remember picking up my Dictaphone, mimicking the cadence and even the accent of my neighbor, and feeling the words begin to flow.

If you're trying to teach a watcher, by far the most effective technique is to get her out of the classroom. Take her away from the manuals, and make her ride shotgun with one of your most experienced performers.

We've seen, in the stories of great managers like Michelle Miller and Judi Langley, that at the very heart of their success lies an appreciation for individuality. This is not to say that managers don't need other skills. They need to be able to hire well, to set expectations, and to interact productively with their own bosses, just to name a few. But what they do—instinctively—is play chess. Mediocre managers assume (or hope) that their employees will all be motivated by the same things and driven by the same goals, that they will desire the same kinds of relationships and learn in roughly the same way. They define the behaviors they expect from people and tell them to work on behaviors that don't come naturally. They praise those who can overcome their natural styles to conform to preset ideas. In short, they believe the manager's job is to mold, or transform, each employee into the perfect version of the role.

Great managers don't try to change a person's style. They never try to push a knight to move in the same way as a bishop. They know that their employees will differ in how they think, how they build relationships, how altruistic they are, how patient they can be, how much of an expert they need to be, how prepared they need to feel, what drives them, what challenges them, and what their goals are. These differences of trait and talent are like blood types: They cut across the superficial variations of race, sex, and age and capture the essential uniqueness of each individual.

Like blood types, the majority of these differences are enduring and resistant to change. A manager's most precious resource is time, and great managers know that the most effective way to invest their time is to identify exactly how each employee is different and then to figure out how best to incorporate those enduring idiosyncrasies into the overall plan.

To excel at managing others, you must bring that insight to your actions and interactions. Always remember that great managing is about release, not transformation. It's about constantly tweaking your environment so that the unique contribution, the unique needs, and the unique style of each employee can be given free rein. Your success as a manager will depend almost entirely on your ability to do this.

Marcus Buckingham is the head of people and performance research at the ADP Research Institute and a co-author of *Nine Lies About Work: A Freethinking Leader's Guide to the Real World* (Harvard Business Review Press, 2019).

CHAPTER 2

Managing Authenticity: The Paradox of Great Leadership

by Rob Goffee and Gareth Jones

Leadership demands the expression of an authentic self. Try to lead like someone else, and you will fail. Employees will not follow someone who invests little of themself in their leadership behaviors. People want to be led by someone "real."

But while the expression of an authentic self is necessary for great leadership, the concept of authenticity is

Excerpted from an article in *Harvard Business Review*, December 2005 (product #R0512E).

often misunderstood, not least by leaders themselves. They often assume that authenticity is an innate quality—that a person is either authentic or not. In fact, authenticity is a quality that others must attribute to you. No leader can look into a mirror and say, "I am authentic." A person cannot be authentic on their own. Authenticity is largely defined by what other people see in you and, as such, can to a great extent be controlled by you. If authenticity were purely an innate quality, there would be little you could do to manage it and, therefore, little you could do to make yourself more effective as a leader.

Let us be absolutely clear: Authenticity is not the product of pure manipulation. It accurately reflects aspects of the leader's inner self, so it can't be an act. But great leaders seem to know which personality traits they should reveal to whom and when. They are like chameleons, capable of adapting to the demands of the situations they face and the people they lead, yet they do not lose their identities in the process. Authentic leaders remain focused on where they are going but never lose sight of where they came from.

There's no one right way to establish and manage your authenticity. But there are conscious steps you can take to help others perceive you as an authentic leader. Some of these steps entail building up knowledge about your true self; some involve learning more about others.

Get to know yourself and your origins better by:

Exploring your autobiography. Familiarize yourself with your identity anchors—the people, places, and events that shaped you. Share these discoveries with others who have had similar experiences.

Returning to your roots. Take a holiday with old friends. Spend time away from the normal trappings of the office.

Avoiding comfort zones. Step out of your routines, seek new adventures, and take some risks.

Getting honest feedback. Ask for 360-degree feedback from close colleagues, friends, family, and so on.

Get to know others better by:

Building a rich picture of your environment. Don't view others as one-dimensional; find out about people's backgrounds, biographies, families, and obsessions.

Removing barriers between yourself and others. Selectively show a weakness or vulnerability that reveals your approachability to your direct reports, assistants, secretaries, and so on.

Empathizing passionately with your people. Care deeply about the work your people do.

Letting others know what's unique (and authentic) about them. Give people feedback that acknowledges and validates their origins.

Connect to the organizational context better by:

Getting the distance right. Be wary of creating the wrong first impressions. Use both your sense of self and your understanding of your origins to connect with, or to separate yourself from, others.

Sharpening your social antennae. Seek out foreign assignments and other experiences to help you detect the subtle social clues that may spell the difference between your success and failure in attracting followers.

Honoring deeply held values and social mores. You are unlikely to make connections by riding roughshod over other cultures' strongly held beliefs.

Developing your resilience. You will inevitably experience setbacks when you expose yourself to new contexts and cultures. Prepare yourself by learning about and understanding your own values.

———

Rob Goffee is a professor emeritus of organizational behavior at the London Business School.

Gareth Jones was a visiting professor at the IE Business School, in Madrid.

CHAPTER 3

Are You a Good Boss—or a Great One?

by Linda A. Hill and Kent Lineback

"Am I good enough?"

"Am I ready? This is my big opportunity, but now I'm not sure I'm prepared."

These thoughts plagued Jason, an experienced manager, as he lay awake one night fretting about a new position he'd taken. For more than five years he had run a small team of developers in Boston. They produced two highly successful lines of engineering textbooks for the education publishing arm of a major media conglomerate. On the strength of his reputation as a great manager

Adapted from an article in *Harvard Business Review*, January–February 2011 (product #R1101K).

of product development, he'd been chosen by the company to take over an online technical-education startup based in London.

Jason arrived at his new office on a Monday morning, excited and confident, but by the end of his first week he was beginning to wonder whether he was up to the challenge. In his previous work he had led people who'd worked together before and required coordination but little supervision. There were problems, of course, but nothing like what he'd discovered in this new venture. Key members of his group barely talked to one another. Other publishers in the company, whose materials and collaboration he desperately needed, angrily viewed his new group as competition. The goals he'd been set seemed impossible—the group was about to miss some early milestones—and a crucial partnership with an outside organization had been badly, perhaps irretrievably, damaged. On top of all that, his boss, who was located in New York, offered little help. "That's why you're there" was the typical response whenever Jason described a problem. By Friday he was worried about living up to the expectations implied in that response.

Do Jason's feelings sound familiar? Such moments of doubt and even fear may and often do come despite years of management experience. Any number of events can trigger them: An initiative you're running isn't going as expected. Your people aren't performing as they should. You hear talk in the group that "the real problem here is lack of leadership." You think you're doing fine until you, like Jason, receive a daunting new assignment. You're given a lukewarm performance review. Or one day you simply realize that you're no longer growing and advancing—you're stuck.

Most Managers Stop Working on Themselves

The whole question of how managers grow and advance is one we've studied, thought about, and lived with for years. As a professor working with high potentials, MBAs, and executives from around the globe, Linda meets people who want to contribute to their organizations and build fulfilling careers. As an executive, Kent has worked with managers at all levels of both private and public organizations. All our experience brings us to a simple but troubling observation: Most bosses reach a certain level of proficiency and stop there—short of what they could and should be.

We've discussed this observation with countless colleagues, who almost without exception have seen what we see: Organizations usually have a few great managers, some capable ones, a horde of mediocre ones, some poor ones, and some awful ones. The great majority of people we work with are well-intentioned, smart, accomplished individuals. Many progress and fulfill their ambitions. But too many derail and fail to live up to their potential. Why? Because they stop working on themselves.

Managers rarely ask themselves, "How good am I?" and "Do I need to be better?" unless they're shocked into it. When did *you* last ask those questions? On the spectrum of great to awful bosses, where do you fall?

Managers in new assignments usually start out receptive to change. The more talented and ambitious ones choose stretch assignments, knowing that they'll have much to learn at first. But as they settle in and lose their fear of imminent failure, they often grow complacent. Every organization has its ways of doing things—policies, standard practices, and unspoken guidelines, such as "promote by seniority" and "avoid conflict." Once they're learned, managers often use them to get by—to "manage" in the worst sense of the word.

It doesn't help that a majority of the organizations we see offer their managers minimal support and rarely press the experienced ones to improve. Few expect more of their leaders than short-term results, which by themselves don't necessarily indicate real management skill.

In our experience, however, the real culprit is neither managerial complacency nor organizational failure: It is a lack of understanding. When bosses are questioned, it's clear that many of them have stopped making progress because they simply *don't know how to.*

Do you understand what's required to become truly effective?

Too often managers underestimate how much time and effort it takes to keep growing and developing. Becoming a great boss is a lengthy, difficult process of learning and change, driven mostly by personal experience. Indeed, so much time and effort are required that you can think of the process as a journey—a journey of years.

What makes the journey especially arduous is that the lessons involved cannot be taught. Leadership is using yourself as an instrument to get things done in the organization, so it is about self-development. There are no secrets and few shortcuts. You and every other manager must learn the lessons yourself, based on your own experience as a boss. If you don't understand the nature of the journey, you're more likely to pause or lose hope and tell yourself, "I can't do this" or "I'm good enough already."

Do you understand what you're trying to attain?

We all know how disorganized, fragmented, and even chaotic every manager's workdays are. Given this reality, which is intensifying as work and organizations become more complex and fluid, how can you as a boss do anything more than cope with what comes at you day by day?

To deal with the chaos, you need a clear underlying sense of what's important and where you and your group want to be in the future. You need a mental model that you can lay over the chaos and into which you can fit all the messy pieces as they come at you. This way of thinking begins with a straightforward definition: Management is responsibility for the performance of a group of people.

It's a simple idea, yet putting it into practice is difficult, because management is *defined* by responsibility but *done* by exerting influence. To influence others you must make a difference not only in what they do but also in the thoughts and feelings that drive their actions. How do you actually do this?

To answer that question, you need an overarching, integrated way of thinking about your work as a manager.

We offer an approach based on studies of management practice, our own observations, and our knowledge of where managers tend to go wrong. We call it the *three imperatives*: Manage yourself. Manage your network. Manage your team.

Is this the only way to describe management? No, of course not. But it's clear, straightforward, and, above all, focused on what managers must actually do. People typically think of "management" as just the third imperative, but today all three are critical to success. Together they encompass the crucial activities that effective managers must perform to influence others. Mastering them is the purpose of your journey.

Manage Yourself

Management begins with you, because who you are as a person, what you think and feel, the beliefs and values that drive your actions, and especially how you connect with others all matter to the people you must influence. Every day those people examine every interaction with you, your every word and deed, to uncover your intentions. They ask themselves, "Can I trust this person?" How hard they work, their level of personal commitment, their willingness to accept your influence, will depend in large part on the qualities they see in you. And their perceptions will determine the answer to this fundamental question every manager must ask: Am I someone who can influence others productively?

Who you are shows up most clearly in the relationships you form with others, especially those for whom you're responsible. It's easy to get those crucial relationships wrong. Effective managers possess the self-awareness and self-management required to get them right.

José, a department head, told us of two managers who worked for him in the marketing department of a large maker of durable goods. Both managers were struggling to deliver the results expected of their groups. Both, it turned out, were creating dysfunctional relationships. One was frankly ambivalent about being "the boss" and hated it when people referred to him that way. He wanted to be liked, so he tried to build close personal relationships. He would say, in effect, "Do what I ask because we're friends." That worked for a while until, for good reasons, he had to turn down one "friend" for promotion and deny another one a bonus. Naturally, those people felt betrayed, and their dissatisfaction began to poison the feelings of everyone else in the group.

The other manager took the opposite approach. With her it was all business. No small talk or reaching out to people as people. For her, results mattered, and she'd been made the boss because she was the one who knew what needed to be done; it was the job of her people to execute. Not surprisingly, her message was always "Do what I say because I'm the boss." She was effective—until people began leaving.

If productive influence doesn't arise from being liked ("I'm your friend!") or from fear ("I'm the boss!"), where does it come from? From people's trust in you as a manager. That trust has two components: belief in your *competence* (you know what to do and how to do it) and belief in your *character* (your motives are good and you want your people to do well).

Trust is the foundation of all forms of influence other than coercion, and you need to conduct yourself with others in ways that foster it. Management really does begin with who you are as a person.

Manage Your Network

We once talked to Kim, the head of a software company division, just as he was leaving a meeting of a task force consisting of his peers. He had proposed a new way of handling interdivisional sales, which he believed would increase revenue by encouraging each division to cross-sell other divisions' products. At the meeting he'd made an extremely well-researched, carefully reasoned, and even compelling case for his proposal—which the group rejected with very little discussion. "How many of these people did you talk to about your proposal before the meeting?" we asked. None, it turned out. "But I anticipated all their questions and objections," he protested, adding with some bitterness, "It's just politics. If they can't see what's good for the company and them, I can't help them."

Many managers resist the need to operate effectively in their organizations' political environments. They consider politics dysfunctional—a sign the organization is broken—and don't realize that it unavoidably arises from three features inherent in all organizations: *division of labor*, which creates disparate groups with disparate and even conflicting goals and priorities; *inter-*

dependence, which means that none of those groups can do their work without the others; and *scarce resources*, for which groups necessarily compete. Obviously, some organizations handle the politics better than others, but conflict and competition among groups are inevitable. How do they get resolved? Through organizational influence. Groups whose managers have influence tend to get what they need; other groups don't.

Unfortunately, many managers deal with conflict by trying to avoid it. "I hate company politics!" they say. "Just let me do my job." But effective managers know they cannot turn away. Instead, with integrity and for good ends, they proactively engage the organization to create the conditions for their success. They build and nurture a broad network of ongoing relationships with those they need and those who need them; that is how they influence people over whom they have no formal authority. They also take responsibility for making their boss, a key member of their network, a source of influence on their behalf.

Manage Your Team

As a manager, Wei worked closely with each of her people, who were spread across the United States and the Far East. But she rarely called a virtual group meeting, and only once had her group met face-to-face. "In my experience," she told us, "meetings online or in person are usually a waste of time. Some people do all the yakking, others stay silent, and not much gets done. It's a lot more efficient for me to work with each person and arrange for them to coordinate when that's necessary." It turned out, though, that she was spending all her time "coordinating," which included a great deal of conflict mediation. People under her seemed to be constantly at odds, vying for the scarce resources they needed to achieve their disparate goals and complaining about what others were or were not doing.

Too many managers overlook the possibilities of creating a real team and managing their people as a whole. They don't realize that managing one-on-one is just not the same as managing a group and that they can influence individual behavior much more effectively through the group, because most of us are social creatures who want to fit in and be accepted as part of the team. How do you make the people who work for you, whether on a project or permanently, into a real team—a group of people who are mutually committed to a common purpose and the goals related to that purpose?

To do collective work that requires varied skills, experience, and knowledge, teams are more creative and productive than groups of individuals who merely cooperate. In a real team, members hold themselves and one another jointly accountable. They share a genuine conviction that they will succeed or fail together. A clear and compelling purpose, and concrete goals and plans based on that purpose, are critical. Without them no group will coalesce into a real team.

Team culture is equally important. Members need to know what's required of them collectively and individually; what the team's values, norms, and standards are; how members are expected to work together (what kind of conflict is acceptable or unacceptable, for example);

and how they should communicate. It's your job to make sure they have all this crucial knowledge.

Effective managers also know that even in a cohesive team they cannot ignore individual members. Every person wants to be a valued member of a group *and* needs individual recognition. You must be able to provide the attention members need, but always in the context of the team.

And finally, effective managers know how to lead a team through the work it does day after day—including the unplanned problems and opportunities that frequently arise—to make progress toward achieving their own and the team's goals.

Be Clear on How You're Doing

The three imperatives will help you influence both those who work for you and those who don't. Most important, they provide a clear and actionable road map for your journey. You must master them to become a fully effective manager.

These imperatives are not simply distinct managerial competencies. They are tightly integrated activities, each of which depends on the others. Getting your person-to-person relationships right is critical to building a well-functioning team and giving its individual members the attention they need. A compelling team purpose, bolstered by clear goals and plans, is the foundation for a strong network, and a network is indispensable for reaching your team's goals.

Knowing where you're going is only the first half of what's required. You also need to know at all times where you are on your journey and what you must do to make progress. We're all aware that the higher you rise in an organization, the less feedback you get about your performance. You have to be prepared to regularly assess yourself.

Too many managers seem to assume that development happens automatically. They have only a vague sense of the goal and of where they stand in relation to it. They tell themselves, "I'm doing all right" or "As I take on more challenges, I'll get better." Consequently, those managers fall short. There's no substitute for routinely taking a look at yourself and how you're doing. (Figure 3-1, "Measuring yourself on the three imperatives," will help you do this.)

Don't be discouraged if you find several areas in which you could do better. No manager will meet all the standards implicit in the three imperatives. The goal is not perfection. It's developing the strengths you need for success and compensating for any fatal shortcomings. Look at your strengths and weaknesses in the context of your organization. What knowledge and skills does it—or will it—need to reach its goals? How can your strengths help it move forward? Given its needs and priorities, what weaknesses must you address right away? The answers become your personal learning goals.

What You Can Do Right Now

Progress will come only from your work experience: from trying and learning, observing and interacting with others, experimenting, and sometimes pushing yourself beyond the bounds of comfort—and then assessing yourself on the three imperatives again and again. Above all, take responsibility for your own development; ultimately, all development is self-development.

You won't make progress unless you consciously act. Before you started a business, you would draw up a business plan broken into manageable steps with milestones; do the same as you think about your journey. Set personal goals. Solicit feedback from others. Take advantage of company training programs. Create a network of trusted advisers, including role models and mentors. Use your strengths to seek out developmental experiences. We know you've heard all this advice before, and it is good advice. But what we find most effective is building the learning into your daily work.

For this purpose we offer a simple approach we call *prep, do, review*.

Prep

Begin each morning with a quick preview of the coming day's events. For each one, ask yourself how you can use it to develop as a manager and in particular how you can work on your specific learning goals. Consider delegating a task you would normally take on yourself and think about how you might do that—to whom, what questions you should ask, what boundaries or limits you should set, what preliminary coaching you might provide. Apply the same thinking during the day when a problem comes up unexpectedly. Before taking any action, step back and consider how it might help you become better. Stretch yourself. If you don't move outside familiar patterns and practice new approaches, you're unlikely to learn.

FIGURE 3-1

Measuring yourself on the three imperatives

		I NEED TO MAKE PROGRESS		THIS IS A STRENGTH	
	Are you performing all the activities necessary to be an effective boss? To get some sense of where you stand, assess yourself on the following questions:				
MANAGE YOURSELF	1. Do you use your formal authority effectively?	**THIS IS A STRENGTH IF** you consider it a useful tool but not your primary means of influencing others. You make clear why you do what you do—and even share your authority with others when possible and appropriate. You focus more on the responsibilities that come with authority than on the personal privileges it provides.	1 2	3	4 5
	2. Do you create thoughtful but not overly personal relationships?	**THIS IS A STRENGTH IF** your relationships are rich in human connections but always focused on the purpose and goals of the team and the organization. You avoid trying to influence people by befriending them.	1 2	3	4 5
	3. Do others trust you as a manager?	**THIS IS A STRENGTH IF** people, particularly your own, believe in your competence, intentions, and values. You demonstrate concern for their individual success.	1 2	3	4 5
	4. Do you exercise your influence ethically?	**THIS IS A STRENGTH IF** you consistently identify stakeholders, weigh their interests, and try to mitigate any harm that your actions may cause as you attempt to accomplish a greater good.	1 2	3	4 5
MANAGE YOUR NETWORK	5. Do you systematically identify those who should be in your network?	**THIS IS A STRENGTH IF** you are always aware of which people and groups you and your team depend on, and vice versa, as circumstances change.	1 2	3	4 5
	6. Do you proactively build and maintain your network?	**THIS IS A STRENGTH IF** you create and sustain relationships with those in your network, connect frequently with them, and support their needs.	1 2	3	4 5
	7. Do you use your network to provide the protection and resources your team needs?	**THIS IS A STRENGTH IF** you protect your team from distractions and misunderstandings, use your network to solve problems inside and outside the team, and secure the funds, people, and other resources it needs.	1 2	3	4 5

			1	2	3	4	5
8. Do you use your network to accomplish your team's goals?	**THIS IS A STRENGTH IF** you form coalitions of network members to support your team's goals and help others in your network achieve theirs. Your network colleagues believe in your competence and character.		1	2	3	4	5
9. Do you define and constantly refine your team's vision for the future?	**THIS IS A STRENGTH IF** you've defined your team's purpose and the goals, strategies, and actions that will take you there. You constantly gather information, discuss your plans with others, and refine your ideas.		1	2	3	4	5
MANAGE YOUR TEAM 10. Do you clarify roles, work rules, team culture, and feedback about performance for your team?	**THIS IS A STRENGTH IF** your people feel a strong sense of "we"—that they're all pulling together toward the same worthwhile goals. They know how they individually contribute and what the team's work involves. They receive regular feedback from you.		1	2	3	4	5
11. Do you know and manage your people as individuals as well as team members?	**THIS IS A STRENGTH IF** you interact equitably with all team members individually. You delegate, strive to help people grow, and constantly assess their performance. You hire people who both fit the team and add diversity, and you deal with performance issues quickly.		1	2	3	4	5
12. Do you use daily activities and problems to pursue the three imperatives?	**THIS IS A STRENGTH IF** you regularly consider how every problem, obligation, or event can help you build your team, make progress on its goals, develop people, and strengthen your network.		1	2	3	4	5

HOW DID YOU DO? Did your responses cover the whole range from 1 to 5? If you consistently assessed yourself at 3 or above, you should be skeptical. In our experience, few bosses merit high ratings across the board. Did you give yourself mostly 3s? Take care not to hide in the middle, telling yourself, "I'm OK—not great, but not failing either." And don't be satisfied to stay there. "I'm not failing" is the watchword of those who are comfortable—and stuck.

Do

Take whatever action is required in your daily work, and as you do, use the new and different approaches you planned. Don't lose your resolve. For example, if you tend to cut off conflict in a meeting, even constructive conflict, force yourself to hold back so that disagreement can be expressed and worked through. Step in only if the discussion becomes personal or points of view are being stifled. The ideas that emerge may lead you to a better outcome.

Review

After the action, examine what you did and how it turned out. This is where learning actually occurs. Reflection is critical, and it works best if you make it a regular practice. For example, set aside time toward the end of each day—perhaps on your commute home. Which actions worked well? What might you have done differently? Replay conversations. Compare what you did with what you might have done if you were the manager you aspire to be. Where did you disappoint yourself, and how did that happen? Did you practice any new behaviors or otherwise make progress on your journey?

Some managers keep notes about how they spent their time, along with thoughts about what they learned. One CEO working on a corporate globalization strategy told us he'd started recording every Friday his reflections about the past week. Within six weeks, he said, he'd developed greater discipline to say no to anything "not on the critical path," which gave him time to spend with key regulators and to jump-start the strategy.

If you still need to make progress on your journey, that should spur you to action, not discourage you. You can become what you want and need to be. But you must take personal responsibility for mastering the three imperatives and assessing where you are now.

Linda A. Hill is the Wallace Brett Donham Professor of Business Administration at Harvard Business School. She is the author of *Becoming a Manager* (Harvard Business Review Press, 2019) and a coauthor of *Being the Boss* (Harvard Business Review Press, 2011) and *Collective Genius* (Harvard Business Review Press, 2014).

Kent Lineback spent many years as a manager and an executive in business and government. He is a coauthor of *Being the Boss* and *Collective Genius*.

Build Trust and Listen

CHAPTER 4

Do You Really Trust Your Team?

by Amy Jen Su

Trust is a frequently used word. Just in the last month, consider how many times you've used it in thinking about your team:

- If I felt more *trust* in her, I'd give her more responsibility.

- One of the goals for our retreat is to build *trust* among employees.

- It's important that other groups in the organization *trust* my team.

Adapted from "Do You Really Trust Your Team? (And Do They Trust You?)," on hbr.org, December 16, 2019 (product #H05BTN).

While we talk a lot about trust, what do we really mean when we make these statements? Why does building trust matter so much? And what can we do as leaders to increase trust on our teams?

The *why* part may be easier to answer. Much has been written about trust and its importance in determining employee engagement, team alignment, and how comfortable a leader is delegating to others.

As to the *what* and *how* parts, trust can be a frustrating action to analyze in that it tends to be a gut feeling for us instead of a concrete choice. This makes it difficult to pinpoint the reasons why we trust one person more than another—and easy to believe there is little we can do to change that. But when we assume that trust is dependent entirely on the behavior of other people, as opposed to our own responses and interactions with those behaviors, we end up falling short as leaders.

To create work environments in which trust can flourish, we first need to understand how it really works: the various ways it can be given, built, and broken. Once we do, we can teach ourselves how to act (and react) in ways that help it grow, even in the most challenging situations. The following questions are designed to help you single out the types of trust that are most lacking between you and your team. If you find that certain areas are especially weak, try taking the suggested steps to strengthen them. You might find that you also help your employees build their capabilities and character along the way.

Trust in Performance

The first three questions address the "harder" aspects of trust: performance-based factors that have a major impact on how you and your team deliver results, make decisions, and show up to the rest of the business.

1. How much do I trust my team members to follow through?

At its most basic level, trust is about the work that needs to get done. To trust someone means to be confident that they will follow through on their responsibilities. I have seen whole teams fail to gain alignment and come to a screeching halt because there is an unspoken annoyance toward one person whom others consider unreliable. This typically occurs when that person isn't holding themselves, or being held, accountable, and it can take place at any level, regardless of title.

As someone in a position of power, you can prevent this. If you want your people to be more dependable and trust one another, as well as you, create an environment that encourages open communication. Here are a few ways to do that:

- **Hold regular one-on-one meetings.** Ask team members to bring a dashboard/catalog of their work. This ensures that part of the time is spent on the important items and not just on fire drills. If they are falling behind in a way that creates risk, encourage them to tell you (and don't shame them). People need to feel safe telling you about their problems, or you won't be able to help resolve them. Sometimes this may mean taking some things off their plate or reprioritizing. Other times it may mean clearing obstacles that are holding them back.

- **Be fair when giving feedback.** Set clear standards for assessing performance at the start of a project. When giving feedback during your one-on-ones, make sure you do so equally based on the standards you originally set. This way everyone will know what is expected of them and be held mutually accountable for their actions.

- **Approach those who may be struggling silently.** Some team members may not feel comfortable approaching you with a problem. Signs that someone may be having a hard time include demotivation, lack of productivity, high stress, or trouble focusing.

2. How much do I trust my team members to bring good judgment?

When you find yourself getting burned out as a result of overinvolvement in other people's projects or because every decision must be approved by you, it's a sign that you need to work on your ability to give trust in this area. By holding trust back, you not only create process restraints for your team but also risk essentially saying to them, "I don't trust you to do good work without me."

There are a few ways you can change your leadership style to rebuild trust in this situation:

- **Good judgment is a muscle—help your team build it.** After making important decisions, talk them through with your team. Explain the subjective and objective criteria you considered, risks and trade-offs you assessed, and stakeholder considerations. This will teach people how and why you make the choices that you do, give them a better understanding of the company's priorities, and demonstrate the factors you would like them to consider when making judgment calls in the future.

- **Acknowledge that failure will happen, and that's OK.** Consider the mistakes you've made in your career and how they've helped you grow into the leader you are today. Give your team that same space. Let them flourish and fail, and when they fail, help them grow from it as opposed to writing them off. This means letting them make big or hard decisions on their own from time to time. Take a back seat in situations where you can bear a little risk. You can always follow up with people after and highlight areas for improvement.

- **When a team member makes a poor judgment call, be curious, not dismissive.** Ask them guiding questions to push their thinking and deepen your understanding of their thought process: What assumptions or criteria underlie your assessment or decision? What risk framework did you apply to this? How will this impact the budget, timing, or work for another group? If they are unable to answer those questions, ask them to come back to you with more information or data to back their argument. Ultimately, this dialogue will allow you to more accurately assess your team member's judgment capabilities and lead you both to a better solution down the line.

3. How much do I trust team members to represent me and the organization?

Your decision to offer team members greater visibility, both internally and externally, is typically drawn from how well you think they will inspire the confidence of key constituencies. This includes showing up with a professional presence, displaying confidence, and being able to engage with others effectively.

If you're hesitant to give certain employees this opportunity, consider why. At the end of the day, your lack of trust could be keeping them from growing and reaching their full potential. To build trust in this area, try doing the following:

- **Set your employees up for success.** Sometimes people don't know the expectations your organization has for engaging professionally with others, and when this happens, it is no wonder they fall short. Prepare them by creating a set of principles outlining the ways in which they should engage with key constituencies within and outside the company. Explain what your function's value proposition is and how that should be communicated to others.

- **Provide coaching and mentoring opportunities to those interested or those who show potential.** One way to do this is to invite team members to observe or participate in executive meetings or presentations with you. As you watch their skills grow, you will not only be building their confidence, but also growing their trust in you as a mentor and your trust in them as a performer.

- **Be clear about who serves as the point person for important contacts.** The more exposure your team members get, the more opportunity there is for confusion to arise around who owns what relationships. Let your team know whether or not you are delegating full relationship ownership to them. If you're not, then discuss the best ways to tag-team the relationship and keep each other in the loop. This way, you can empower people without feeling like they are stepping on your toes.

Trust in Principles

The next three questions address "softer" aspects of trust: principle-based factors that have a real impact on your team's engagement and satisfaction, as well as on the perceived integrity of your team by those with whom they work.

1. How much do I trust my team members to practice an appropriate level of discretion?

Because knowledge sharing and "being in the know" is a powerful way to connect with others, it can be challenging for people to decipher which information is most useful to share and which information is best kept private. More often than not, this is why people unintentionally breach confidences.

But trust in this area is so important. When you start overediting yourself due to a lack of confidence in your team's discretion, you risk holding back information that will help them do their jobs well, and their performance can suffer as a result. There are some things you can do to build a strong foundation of trust in this case:

- **Educate your team.** Let them know from day one that not everything you share internally is free game, particularly information that is protected by nondisclosure agreements or that creates a conflict of interest with another party or customers. Provide them with examples of exactly what you mean so that they can easily recognize and avoid dangerous situations. If you share something sensitive during a meeting and you want it kept private, don't assume people can read your mind. Just say so.

- **Set ground rules.** At the beginning of team retreats, let people know that any personal information that is shared should be treated respectfully. By setting these standards from the start, you will be showing your team that you respect their privacy and take it seriously. Further, you will be helping to build a culture of trust, and your team will be more likely to value the privacy of others and the organization at large when necessary.

- **Be an accessible resource.** If your direct reports are unsure about gray areas, especially during times of change or uncertainty, advise them to come to you or HR for counsel. It's important for people to know you are available to support them.

2. Do I trust my team members to respect the psychological safety of others?

Our brains are trained to constantly scan for and avoid people who threaten our sense of well-being. When we perceive someone who is a "threat," we either attack or retreat, and when we retreat, we lose access to important skills such as listening, asking questions, and speaking up about our ideas. This is why it's so important to maintain a positive team culture. If people feel psychologically unsafe due to one bad egg, they likely won't reach their full potential.

If there is a lack of psychological safety on your team, use the following steps to build, or rebuild, it. (For more on psychological safety, see chapter 6.)

- **Model healthy conflict.** When you and a team member have a disagreement, whether in a one-on-one or in a larger meeting, approach it respectfully by giving the other person space to voice their point of view. It's important that you welcome and acknowledge opinions that are different from your own—even if it means engaging in civil debate. Doing so shows the rest of your team that it's possible to share opposing perspectives with a tone and approach that is constructive.

- **Have zero tolerance for bullying.** If you witness a team member engaging in blatantly rude behavior—such as interrupting, dismissing, steamrolling, condescending, or using derogatory language toward others—address it immediately. Almost every team I have worked with has, at one point or another, had a toxic member who impacts the camaraderie and collaboration of the group. Rather than avoiding the elephant in the room or forcing everyone to work around that person, you, as the leader, must hold them accountable for their behavior, even if they are a strong performer.

- **Create a culture of appreciation.** Reinforce and capitalize on each person's strengths, perspectives, and contributions to the team by calling out their achievements and wins in meetings or group settings. A culture that only focuses on negative feedback or what people are doing wrong can leave your team feeling discouraged or defensive.

3. How much do I trust my team members' underlying intentions and motivations?

Ultimately, we need our teams to work toward doing what's best for the organization. This can be tricky, as personal motivations are often at play, and our assessment of them can either increase or decrease our trust in others.

While you can't control a person's intentions, there are things you can do to encourage and reward team play:

- **Break down silos.** Try to manage less by "hub and spoke." Instead, be intentional about activities that build team esprit de corps. Remind people that they are part of a larger collective by creating shared team goals and connecting them to the bigger picture. Explain how each person's work influences the performance of the larger organization.

- **Consider that people may not be the problem.** Sometimes performance management and incentive systems are the real issue. Ask yourself: Do our compensation systems only reward individual contributions? Is there anywhere in the performance management system where we can applaud or address team players?

- **Be willing to have a direct conversation.** Don't reward bad behavior. If someone is overly self-absorbed, explain that they are hurting, not helping, themselves. Remind them that leadership roles require cross-functional and team collaboration and that their success will be determined, in part, by how well they work with others.

As you continue to think about how to increase trust among your team and the best ways to create an environment in which it can flourish, return to these six questions. In time, you may find that you are able to more quickly identify pain points that you can help resolve. When you give trust, you not only empower others but also develop the individuals on your team into stronger contributors, and in doing so, you empower yourself as a leader.

———————

Amy Jen Su is a cofounder and managing partner of Paravis Partners, a premier executive coaching and leadership development firm. For the past two decades, she has coached CEOs, executives, and rising stars in organizations. She is the author of *The Leader You Want to Be: Five Essential Principles for Bringing Out Your Best Self—Every Day* (Harvard Business Review Press, 2019), and a coauthor of *Own the Room: Discover Your Signature Voice to Master Your Leadership Presence* (Harvard Business Review Press, 2013) with Muriel Maignan Wilkins.

CHAPTER 5

Open Up to Your Team—Without Oversharing

by Liz Fosslien and Mollie West Duffy

In the age of social sharing, people who work together know more and more about one another. In general, this is a good thing for peers and leaders. Research shows our brains respond positively to people when we feel a personal connection with them.[1] We try harder, perform better, and are kinder to our colleagues. Command-and-control management is on its way out, and bosses who practice empathy and make an effort to connect with their subordinates are in.

Adapted from "How Leaders Can Open Up to Their Teams Without Oversharing," on hbr.org, February 8, 2019 (product #H04MR7).

This willingness in leaders to be open and honest, even if it makes them vulnerable, is important because it builds trust—people can easily sense inauthenticity. We tend to assume that leaders are marketing to us. If a leader never shows emotion, that conviction only becomes stronger. But when a leader reveals a more personal side to herself, and we sense that it is authentic, we feel a connection and are more likely to believe her words.

However, people who *overdo* this accomplish just the opposite and can end up completely undermining themselves. If leaders share information that suggests they are not up to the task—for example, "I'm scared, and I have no idea what to do right now"—there is a good chance their team will take on that same emotion or, worse, lose faith in their ability to lead. People in charge have to think longer and harder than the rest of us about when to be transparent because they have more eyes on them. Every time they are vulnerable (or are not vulnerable), their reports are watching and analyzing their words and actions for a deeper meaning.

So, when does sharing become oversharing? We argue that the way to find a balance between the two is to be *selectively vulnerable*—or open up to your team while still prioritizing their boundaries, as well as your own.

This issue often presents itself when there are new initiatives or changes in an organization. We typically find leaders asking themselves how much of their own worries they should reveal when leading their team down a challenging or unfamiliar road. The best leaders are honest about how they feel while simultaneously presenting a clear path forward. Here's how to do it.

Figure yourself out

The best leaders are able to hit a pause button when they become emotional. Instead of immediately acting, ask yourself, "What exactly am I feeling? Why? What is the need behind this emotion?" For example, an average manager might say she feels irritable about a project because the workload is annoying, but a great manager will take the time to reflect on this emotion. In doing so, she might realize the root cause of her irritability is anxiety about meeting a deadline.

Regulate your emotions

Once you identify your feelings, you need to know how to manage them. This is as important as managing your reports. What you consider a momentary bad mood can ruin someone's day. Reactive, hot-tempered managers are hurtful, demoralizing, and the main reason people quit jobs. Research shows that employees confronted by an angry manager are less willing to work hard—especially if they don't understand where the anger is coming from.[2] But when managers control their words and body language during tense situations, their reports' stress levels drop significantly. "An important part of being a leader is understanding how much weight the people around you can bear," Laszlo Bock, founder and CEO of Humu and former head of HR at Google, told us. "You can't burden your employees with more than they can carry, or expect them to hold you up all the time."

Address your feelings without becoming emotionally leaky

We're often worse at hiding our feelings than we think. If you're frustrated or upset, your employees will most likely pick up on your bad mood and might assume that they are responsible for it. "The idea that you're never going to have a bad day as a boss is bullshit," Kim Scott, author of *Radical Candor*, told us. "The best thing to do is to cop to it. Say to your team, 'I'm having a bad day, and I'm trying my best not to take it out on you. But if it seems like I'm having a bad day, I am. But it's not because of you that I'm having a bad day. The last thing I want is for my bad day to make your day worse." You don't have to go into more detail, but acknowledging your feelings helps you avoid creating unnecessary anxiety among your reports.

Provide a path forward

When you're tackling a challenging project, practice how you're going to share your emotions with your team, and make sure you do so with intention. Dumping your feelings onto them in a reactive or unthoughtful way leaves a lot of room for misinterpretation. Aim to be realistic but optimistic. A good formula to follow is: *Because of _____, I'm feeling _____ and _____. But here's what I'm planning to do next to make it better: _____. And here's what I need from you: _____. What do you need from me?* This will help you address your anxiety without projecting negative emotions onto your team.

"It's a promise to work toward a solution *in spite of* emotions," says Jerry Colonna, former venture capitalist and coach, also known as the "CEO Whisperer."

Avoid oversharing

A good rule of thumb for figuring out if you're about to overshare is to ask yourself: "How would I feel if my manager said this to me?" If it's something that you'd be thankful to hear, chances are your reports will feel similarly. If it's something that would give you pause, err on the side of caution. Be curious about your own intentions. Are you sharing from a place of authenticity, or are you trying to fabricate a connection with others? Sometimes we overshare personal experiences just to feel close with someone else. But often, this is not useful or effective.

Read the room

If you think members of your team might be feeling anxious about the project, it's OK to surface those feelings to help them feel less isolated. For example, if everyone has been working long hours to meet an impending deadline, you might say something like, "I'm feeling a little tired today, but I'm grateful for how well we've worked together and that we're set to send the client a proposal we can all be proud of." Again, always try to pair realism with optimism, and share when you sense it will be helpful to others.

Finding the right balance between sharing and oversharing is not easy. But with practice, it can be done. As a leader, it's your job to understand the powerful role your emotions play, and to harness them in ways that will help your team succeed.

———————

Liz Fosslien is the head of content at Humu, a company that nudges people toward better work habits, unlocking the potential of individuals, teams, and organizations. She has designed and led sessions related to emotions at work for audiences including TED, LinkedIn, Google, Viacom, and Spotify. Liz's writing and illustrations have been featured by the *Economist*, Freakonomics, and NPR.

Mollie West Duffy is an organizational development expert and consultant. She was previously an organizational design lead at global innovation firm IDEO and a research associate for the former dean of Harvard Business School, Nitin Nohria, and renowned strategy professor Michael E. Porter. She's written for *Fast Company, Quartz, Stanford Social Innovation Review, Entrepreneur*, and other digital outlets. Liz and Mollie are the authors of the book *No Hard Feelings: The Secret Power of Embracing Emotions at Work*. Follow them on Twitter or Instagram @lizandmollie.

NOTES

1. Richard E. Boyatzis et al., "Examination of the Neural Substrates Activated in Memories of Experiences with Resonant and Dissonant Leaders," *Leadership Quarterly 23*, no. 2 (2012): 259–272, https://www.sciencedirect.com/science/article/pii/S1048984311001263.

2. Lukas F. Koning and Gerben A. Van Kleef, "How Leaders' Emotional Displays Shape Followers' Organizational Citizenship Behavior," *Leadership Quarterly* 26, no. 4 (2015): 489–501, https://www.sciencedirect.com/science/article/pii/S1048984315000296.

High-Performing Teams Need Psychological Safety

by Laura Delizonna

"There's no team without trust," says Paul Santagata, head of industry at Google. He knows the results of the tech giant's massive two-year study on team performance, which revealed that the highest-performing teams have one thing in common: psychological safety, the belief that you won't be punished when you make a

Adapted from "High-Performing Teams Need Psychological Safety. Here's How to Create It," on hbr.org, August 24, 2017 (product #H03TK7).

mistake.[1] Studies show that psychological safety allows for moderate risk-taking, speaking your mind, creativity, and sticking your neck out without fear of having it cut off—just the types of behavior that lead to market breakthroughs.

Ancient evolutionary adaptations explain why psychological safety is both fragile and vital to success in uncertain, interdependent environments.[2] The brain processes a provocation by a boss, competitive coworker, or dismissive subordinate as a life-or-death threat. The amygdala, the alarm bell in the brain, ignites the fight-or-flight response, hijacking higher brain centers. This "act first, think later" brain structure shuts down perspective and analytical reasoning. Quite literally, just when we need it most, we lose our minds. While that fight-or-flight reaction may save us in life-or-death situations, it handicaps the strategic thinking needed in today's workplace.

Twenty-first-century success depends on another system—the broaden-and-build mode of positive emotion, which allows us to solve complex problems and foster cooperative relationships. Barbara Fredrickson at the University of North Carolina has found that positive emotions like trust, curiosity, confidence, and inspiration broaden the mind and help us build psychological, social, and physical resources. We become more open-minded, resilient, motivated, and persistent when we feel safe. Humor increases, as does solution finding and divergent thinking—the cognitive process underlying creativity.

When the workplace feels challenging but not threatening, teams can sustain the broaden-and-build mode. Oxytocin levels in our brains rise, eliciting trust and trust-making behavior. This is a huge factor in team success, as Santagata attests: "In Google's fast-paced, highly demanding environment, our success hinges on the ability to take risks and be vulnerable in front of peers."

So how can you increase psychological safety on your own team? Try replicating the steps that Santagata took with his:

1. Approach conflict as a collaborator, not an adversary

We humans hate losing even more than we love winning. A perceived loss triggers attempts to reestablish fairness through competition, criticism, or disengagement, which is a form of workplace-learned helplessness. Santagata knows that true success is a win-win outcome, so when conflicts come up, he avoids triggering a fight-or-flight reaction by asking, "How could we achieve a mutually desirable outcome?"

2. Speak human to human

Underlying every team's who-did-what confrontation are universal needs such as respect, competence, social status, and autonomy. Recognizing these deeper needs naturally elicits trust and promotes positive language and behaviors. Santagata reminded his team that even in the most contentious negotiations, the other party is just like them and aims to walk away happy. He led them through a reflection called "Just Like Me," which asks you to consider:

- This person has beliefs, perspectives, and opinions, just like me.

- This person has hopes, anxieties, and vulnerabilities, just like me.

- This person has friends, family, and perhaps children who love them, just like me.

- This person wants to feel respected, appreciated, and competent, just like me.

- This person wishes for peace, joy, and happiness, just like me.

3. Anticipate reactions and plan countermoves

"Thinking through in advance how your audience will react to your messaging helps ensure your content will be heard, versus your audience hearing an attack on their identity or ego," explains Santagata.

Skillfully confront difficult conversations head-on by preparing for likely reactions. For example, you may need to gather concrete evidence to counter defensiveness when discussing hot-button issues. Santagata asks himself, "If I position my point in this manner, what are the possible objections, and how would I respond to those counterarguments?" He says, "Looking at the discussion from this third-party perspective exposes weaknesses in my positions and encourages me to rethink my argument."

Specifically, he asks:

- What are my main points?

- What are three ways my listeners are likely to respond?

- How will I respond to each of those scenarios?

4. Replace blame with curiosity

If team members sense that you're trying to blame them for something, you become their saber-toothed tiger. Research by John Gottman at the University of Washington shows that blame and criticism reliably escalate conflict, leading to defensiveness and—eventually—to disengagement.[3] The alternative to blame is curiosity. If you believe you already know what the other person is thinking, then you're not ready to have a conversation. Instead, adopt a learning mindset, knowing you don't have all the facts. Here's how:

- State the problematic behavior or outcome as an observation, and use factual, neutral language. For example, "In the past two months there's been a noticeable drop in your participation during meetings and progress appears to be slowing on your project."

- Engage them in an exploration. For example, "I imagine there are multiple factors at play. Perhaps we could uncover what they are together?"

- Ask for solutions. The people who are responsible for creating a problem often hold the keys to solving it. That's why a positive outcome typically depends on their input and buy-in. Ask directly, "What do you think needs to happen here?" Or, "What would be your ideal scenario?" Another question leading to solutions is: "How could I support you?"

5. Ask for feedback on delivery

Asking for feedback on how you delivered your message disarms your opponent, illuminates blind spots in communication skills, and models fallibility, which increases trust in leaders.[4] Santagata closes difficult conversations with these questions:

- What worked and what didn't work in my delivery?

- How did it feel to hear this message?

- How could I have presented it more effectively?

For example, Santagata asked about his delivery after giving his senior manager tough feedback. His manager replied, "This could have felt like a punch in the stomach, but you presented reasonable evidence and that made me want to hear more. You were also eager to discuss the challenges I had, which led to solutions."

6. Measure psychological safety

Santagata periodically asks his team how safe they feel and what could enhance their feeling of safety. In addition, his team routinely takes surveys on psychological safety and other team dynamics.[5] Some teams at Google include questions such as, "How confident are you that you won't receive retaliation or criticism if you admit an error or make a mistake?"

If you create this sense of psychological safety on your own team starting now, you can expect to see higher levels of engagement, increased motivation to tackle difficult problems, more learning and development opportunities, and better performance.

———————

Laura Delizonna is an executive coach, instructor at Stanford University, international speaker, and founder of delizonna.com.

NOTES

1. Julia Rozovsky, "The Five Keys to a Successful Google Team," Re:Work, Google blog, November 17, 2015, https://rework.withgoogle.com/blog/five-keys-to-a-successful-google-team/.

2. Amy Edmondson, "Psychological Safety and Learning Behavior in Work Teams," *Administrative Science Quarterly* 44, no. 2 (1999): 350–383.

3. Kyle Benson, "Transforming Criticism into Wishes: A Recipe for Successful Conflict," Gottman Institute, May 17, 2017, https://www.gottman.com/blog/transforming-criticism-into-wishes-a-recipe-for-successful-conflict/.

4. Bradley P. Owens, Wade Rowatt, and Alan L. Wilkins, "Exploring the Relevance and Implication of Humility in Organizations," in *The Oxford Handbook of Positive Organizational Scholarship*, ed. Gretchen M. Spreitzer and Kim S. Cameron (New York: Oxford University Press, 2011).

5. Amy Edmondson, "Team Learning and Psychological Safety Survey," Measurement Instrument Database for the Social Sciences, n.d., https://www.midss.org/content/team-learning-and-psychological-safety-survey.

CHAPTER 7

How to Handle a Disagreement on Your Team

by Jeanne Brett and Stephen B. Goldberg

When you're leading a collaborative project, you can't always ensure that everyone will get along. Given competing interests, needs, and agendas, you might even have two people who vehemently disagree. What's your role as the boss in a situation like this? Should you get involved or leave them to solve their own problems?

Ideally, you'll be able to coach your colleagues to talk to one another and resolve their conflict without involving you, making clear that their disagreement is harmful

---

Adapted from content posted on hbr.org, July 10, 2017 (product #H03RNN).

to them and the organization. But that's not always possible. In these situations, we believe it's important to intervene, not as a boss but as a mediator. To be sure, you won't be a neutral, independent mediator since you have some stake in the outcome, but you're likely to be more effective in meeting everybody's interests—yours, theirs, and the organization's—if you use your mediation skills rather than your authority.

Why rely on mediation and not your authority?

Your colleagues are more likely to own the decision and follow through with it if they're involved in making it. If you dictate what they should do, they will have learned nothing about resolving conflict themselves. Rather, they will have become more dependent on you to figure out their disputes for them. Plus, you might not even have the formal authority to intervene.

Of course, there will be times when you'll have to put aside your mediator role and decide how the conflict will be resolved—for example, if major departmental or company policy issues are involved, there is imminent danger, or all other avenues have failed to resolve the conflict—but those occasions are few and far between.

What if your colleagues expect you to step in as the leader?

Your first move is to recognize your authority, but explain the mediation process you have in mind. You might tell your colleagues that although you have the authority to impose an outcome on them, you hope that together you can find a resolution that works for everyone. You could also tell them that when the three of you are together, they should devote their energy to reaching agreement, rather than trying to persuade you about which of their views should prevail.

Should you initially meet with each colleague separately or jointly?

There are pros and cons to both approaches. The goal is to understand both of their positions (what one is claiming and the other rejecting) and their interests (why they are making and rejecting the claims).

Conflict often carries with it a heavy dose of emotion. One or both of your colleagues may be seriously angry. One or both may feel intimidated by the other. Meeting with each separately will give the angry colleague an opportunity to vent, give you a chance to reassure the intimidated colleague that you will listen, and may surface information ultimately useful to resolving the conflict— information that colleagues either haven't shared with each other or haven't heard if shared.

If you first sit down with them separately, don't focus the discussion on how to resolve the conflict, but rather on gaining an understanding of the disagreement and convincing each that you are willing to listen and anxious to understand their concerns.

Research has shown that initial separate meetings are more successful if the manager spends time building empathy and gaining an understanding of the problem.[1] There will be plenty of time in subsequent meetings to talk about how to resolve the conflict. Also be sure in this initial meeting that you are using empathy ("That must have been really hard for you") and not sympathy ("I feel sorry for what you have been through"). An expression of empathy is respectful but relatively neutral and it does not imply support for the person's position.

The risk in starting separately is that each colleague may think that the other is going to use that meeting to sway you to the other's perspective. You can avoid this by explaining that the purpose of the meeting is to understand both sides of what is going on, not to form an opinion on who is right and who is wrong.

Meeting jointly at first has its upsides too. Giving each a chance to do some controlled venting in a joint session may clear the air between them. You should check with both before proposing this approach since you want to be sure that they can engage in such a session without losing their composure, making resolution even more difficult. And be sure to set some ground rules—each will have a turn with no interruptions, for example—before you begin and be prepared to tightly control the session and even break it off if you cannot control it; otherwise it can turn brutal.

Another good reason to have your colleagues meet together is that ultimately, they need to own the resolution of their conflict and they need to develop the ability to talk to each other when future conflicts arise. Of course, the risk in meeting jointly is that you cannot control the process and the meeting only escalates the conflict.

Keep in mind that you don't have to pick one mode of meeting and stick with it throughout the process. You can switch between modes. However, our research suggests that starting separately and building empathy and then moving to joint is more effective in resolving conflict than starting jointly and then meeting separately. [2]

What should you accomplish in your first meeting?

Whether you're meeting together or not, there are several things you want to do in the initial meeting. Explain that you see your role as helping them find a mutually acceptable resolution to their conflict, but also to ensure that the resolution does not have negative implications for the team or the organization. Make clear that deciding whether a particular agreement is acceptable requires their buy-in and yours. And then set out some rules for whenever you meet together. For example, treat each with respect and don't interrupt.

The goal of the initial meeting is to have them leave with emotions abated and feeling respected by you, if not yet by each other. With that done, you can then bring them together (if you didn't meet jointly the first time) and focus on getting the information that you all need in order to resolve the conflict.

What information do you need to draw out in subsequent meetings?

In order to resolve the conflict, you'll need to know from both people their positions (what each wants), interests (why each is taking that position, how the position reflects their needs and concerns), and priorities (what is more and less important to each and why).

You can gather this information by doing several things: asking "why?" or "why not?" questions to uncover the interests that underlie their positions, listening carefully to identify those interests, and reformulating what you think you understand about one colleague's interests to make sure you understand and that the other colleague also is hearing them.

What are the pitfalls to avoid?

There are several ways that these discussions can go wrong. For one, either colleague can try to convince you that their view of the facts is the only correct view, that their position is the "right" one, or that they should prevail because they have more power. We call these facts, rights, and power arguments, and they are detrimental because they distract everyone from seeking a resolution that will satisfy everyone's interests.

The facts argument is an interesting one. Both colleagues may have been at the same scene, but each remembers it differently. They both think that if they could only convince you and their colleague of their view of the facts, the conflict would be over. The problem is that even if you had been there, it is counterproductive to try to convince others of your view, because without new credible information, they are unlikely to change their minds about what happened. The best approach to closing this trap is to agree to disagree and move on.

Arguments about rights may come in the form of appeals to fairness or past practices. The problem is that for every rights argument one colleague makes, the other can make a different one that supports their own position. What one party views as fair, the other views as unfair, and vice versa. If they start to invoke fairness, suggest that the discussion be put aside temporarily while you jointly search for information that might be useful in resolving the conflict.

Power arguments are basically threats: *If you don't agree to my position, I will . . .* Being threatened turns people defensive and distrustful, which makes them more reluctant to share information about positions, interests, and priorities. If one person issues a threat, explicit or implicit, remind your colleagues of the ground rules of respect. You might also repeat what you are trying to do—share relevant information to get to a resolution—and mention that a discussion of what one will do if there is no settlement is counterproductive at this point.

How can you move forward toward an agreement?

Finding potential settlements may be easy if, in the process of helping your colleagues understand their different positions and interests, it becomes clear that this conflict was just a misunderstanding or that there is a way forward that respects both parties' interests. If it becomes apparent that their interests are as much in conflict as their positions, finding a settlement may be more difficult, but don't give up.

Our research shows there are several ways to facilitate an agreement in this situation. Surprisingly often, parties can simply agree on how they are going to interact or address the issues in the future. They put the past behind them, accepting that past practice wasn't working for one or the other or both and move forward together. This can be tricky, though. Sometimes one might be willing to engage in a future-based agreement like this but not trust the other to follow through on it. In those cases, where uncertainty is a concern, you can try one of these types of agreements:

- **Limited duration.** Agreements that try something for a limited time and then evaluate before continuing.

- **Contingent.** Agreements that depend on a future event *not* happening. If the future event does happen, an alternative agreement takes effect.

- **Non–precedent-setting.** Agreements that protect against risk by parties agreeing that the settlement will not set a precedent in the event a similar conflict arises in the future.

It's best if your colleagues can propose resolutions that meet their own and the other's interests. You may be able to coach them into making such proposals by summarizing the interests and priorities as you've heard them. You can then ask each colleague to make a proposal that takes into account the interests and priorities of the other. Discourage each from making unrealistic proposals that would offend the other. You might warn them not to make an offer they cannot reasonably justify, because doing so will compromise their credibility.

If, despite everyone's efforts, you can't reach an agreement, you might need to speak with each colleague separately about the consequences of not reaching a resolution. You can ask, "What do you think will happen if you don't reach agreement?" The answer, of course, is they don't know. The only way to keep control over the outcome of the conflict is to resolve it themselves.

If there is still no settlement at this point, you may need to shed your mediator role and, as the leader, impose an outcome that is in the best interests of the organization. Be sure to explain your reasoning and make clear this isn't your desired path. You might also point out that your goal in having them work hard in resolving the dispute on their own was that they would be better equipped to do so in the future, and that goal hasn't been fully accomplished. But don't let them walk away thinking their relationship is doomed. Give them both feedback on what they might do differently next time, making clear that when they butt heads again, you'll expect them to manage it on their own.

Jeanne Brett is professor emeritus at the Kellogg School of Management at Northwestern University. She is the author of *Negotiating Globally.*

Stephen B. Goldberg is a professor of law emeritus at Northwestern Pritzker School of Law, where he taught negotiation, mediation, and arbitration. He is also an experienced mediator and arbitrator.

NOTES

1. Roderick I. Swaab and Jeanne M. Brett, "Caucus with Care: The Impact of Pre-Mediation Caucuses on Conflict Resolution," IACM 2007 Meetings Paper, January 6, 2008, https://papers.ssrn.com/sol3/papers.cfm?abstract_id=1080622.

2. Stephen B. Goldberg et al., *How Mediation Works* (Bingley, UK: Emerald Publishing, 2017).

CHAPTER 8

What Great Listeners Actually Do

by Jack Zenger and Joseph Folkman

Chances are you think you're a good listener. People's appraisal of their listening ability is much like their assessment of their driving skills in that the great bulk of adults think they're above average.

In our experience, most people think good listening comes down to doing three things:

- Not talking when others are speaking

- Letting others know you're listening through facial expressions and verbal sounds ("mm-hmm")

Adapted from content posted on hbr.org, July 14, 2016 (product #H030DC).

- Being able to repeat what others have said, practically word for word

In fact, much management advice on listening suggests doing these very things—encouraging listeners to remain quiet, nod and "mm-hmm" encouragingly, and then repeat back to the talker something like, "So, let me make sure I understand. What you're saying is . . ." However, recent research that we conducted suggests that these behaviors fall far short of describing good listening skills.

We analyzed data describing the behavior of 3,492 participants in a development program designed to help managers become better coaches. As part of this program, their coaching skills were rated by others in 360-degree assessments. We identified those who were perceived as being the most effective listeners (the top 5%). We then compared the best listeners to the average of all other people in the data set and identified the 20 items showing the largest significant difference. With those results in hand, we identified the differences between great and average listeners and analyzed the data to determine what characteristics their colleagues identified as the behaviors that made them outstanding listeners.

We found some surprising conclusions, along with some qualities we expected to hear. We grouped them into four main findings:

- **Good listening is much more than being silent while the other person talks.** To the contrary, people perceive the best listeners to be those who periodically ask questions that promote discovery and insight. These questions gently challenge old assumptions but do so in a constructive way. Sitting there silently nodding does not provide sure evidence that a person is listening, but asking a good question tells the speaker the listener has not only heard what was said but comprehended it well enough to want additional information. Good listening was consistently seen as a two-way dialogue, rather than a one-way "speaker versus hearer" interaction. The best conversations were active.

- **Good listening included interactions that build a person's self-esteem.** The best listeners made the conversation a positive experience for the other party, which doesn't happen when the listener is passive (or, for that matter, critical). Good listeners made the other person feel supported and conveyed confidence in them. Good listening was characterized by the creation of a safe environment in which issues and differences could be discussed openly.

- **Good listening was seen as a cooperative conversation.** In these interactions, feedback flowed smoothly in both directions with neither party becoming defensive about comments the other made. By contrast, poor listeners were seen as competitive—as listening only to identify errors in reasoning or logic, using their silence as a chance to prepare their next response. That might make you an excellent debater, but it doesn't make you a good listener. Good listeners may challenge assumptions and disagree, but the person being listened to feels the listener is trying to help, not wanting to win an argument.

- **Good listeners tended to make suggestions.** Good listening invariably included some feedback provided in a way that others would accept and that opened up alternative paths to consider. This finding somewhat surprised us, since it's not uncommon to hear complaints that "So-and-so didn't listen; he just jumped in and tried to solve the problem." Perhaps what the data is telling us is that making suggestions is not itself the problem; it may be the skill with which those suggestions are made. Another possibility is that we're more likely to accept suggestions from people we already think are good listeners. (Someone who is silent for the whole conversation and then jumps in with a suggestion may not be seen as credible. Someone who seems combative or critical and then tries to give advice may not be seen as trustworthy.)

While many of us have thought of being a good listener as being like a sponge that absorbs what the other person is saying, instead what these findings show is that good listeners are like trampolines. They are someone you can bounce ideas off of—and rather than absorbing your ideas and energy, they amplify, energize, and clarify your thinking. They make you feel better, not by merely passively absorbing, but by actively supporting. This lets you gain energy and height, just like someone jumping on a trampoline.

Of course, there are different levels of listening. Not every conversation requires the highest levels of listening, but many conversations would benefit from greater focus and listening skill. Consider which level of listening you'd like to aim for:

Level 1

The listener creates a safe environment in which difficult, complex, or emotional issues can be discussed.

Level 2

The listener clears away distractions like phones and laptops, focusing attention on the other person and making appropriate eye contact. This behavior not only affects how you are perceived as the listener, but immediately influences the listener's *own* attitudes and inner feelings. Acting the part changes how you feel inside. This in turn makes you a better listener.

Level 3

The listener seeks to understand the substance of what the other person is saying. They capture ideas, ask questions, and restate issues to confirm that their understanding is correct.

Level 4

The listener observes nonverbal cues, such as facial expressions, perspiration, respiration rates, gestures, posture, and numerous other subtle body language signals. It is estimated that 80% of what we communicate comes from these signals. It sounds strange to some, but you listen with your eyes as well as your ears.

Level 5

The listener increasingly understands the other person's emotions and feelings about the topic at hand and identifies and acknowledges them. The listener empathizes with and validates those feelings in a supportive, nonjudgmental way.

Level 6

The listener asks questions that clarify assumptions the other person holds and helps the other person see the issue in a new light. This could include the listener injecting some thoughts and ideas about the topic that could be useful to the other person. However, good listeners never highjack the conversation to make themselves or their issues become the subject of the discussion.

Each of the levels builds on the others; thus, if you've been criticized for offering solutions rather than listening, it may mean you need to attend to some of the other levels (such as clearing away distractions or empathizing) before your proffered suggestions can be appreciated.

We suspect that in being a good listener, most of us are more likely to stop short rather than go too far. The highest and best form of listening comes in playing the same role for the other person that a trampoline plays for a child. It gives energy, acceleration, height, and amplification. These are the hallmarks of great listening.

Jack Zenger is the CEO of Zenger/Folkman, a leadership development consultancy. He is a coauthor of the book *The New Extraordinary Leader: Turning Good Managers into Great Leaders*. Follow him on Twitter @jhzenger.

Joseph Folkman is the president of Zenger/Folkman. He is a coauthor of the book *Speed: How Leaders Accelerate Successful Execution*. Follow him on Twitter @joefolkman.

They are the coauthors of the October 2011 HBR article "Making Yourself Indispensable."

Give Feedback and Motivate

CHAPTER 9

Give Your Team More-Effective Positive Feedback

by Christine Porath

Research shows that one of the best ways to help employees thrive is to give them feedback. It's one of the primary levers leaders have to increase a sense of learning and vitality.[1] Giving your direct reports regular updates on personal performance, as well as on how the business is doing, helps them feel valued. Negative or directive feedback provides guidance, leading people to become, over time, more certain about their behavior and more confident in their competence.

Adapted from content posted on hbr.org, October 25, 2016 (product #H037PM).

Highlighting an employee's strengths can help generate a sense of accomplishment and motivation. A Gallup survey on the state of the American manager found that 67% of employees whose bosses focused on their strengths were fully engaged in their work, as compared with only 31% of employees whose bosses focused on their weaknesses. IBM's WorkTrends survey of over 19,000 workers in 26 countries, across industries and thousands of organizations, revealed that the engagement level of employees who receive recognition is almost three times higher than the engagement level of those who do not. The same survey showed that employees who receive recognition are also far less likely to quit. Recognition has been shown to increase happiness at work in general and is tied to cultural and business results, such as job satisfaction and retention.

Offering positive feedback can generate wins for managers, too. High performers offer more positive feedback to peers; in fact, high-performing teams share nearly six times more positive feedback than average teams.[2] Meanwhile, low-performing teams share nearly twice as much negative feedback as average teams.

Consider which of your team members' positive contributions you currently take for granted. Make a list and start praising team members for their strengths when you see them in action—and try to catch people at it in the moment. The more specific you are, the better. The more you notice what's meaningful to a person, the greater your potential impact will be. Some people prefer a pat on the back in private; others want to bask in the glory of a crowd.

If you don't tend to give much feedback, start scheduling one-on-one meetings. Tell each individual what you want them to start, stop, and continue doing. See if you can list a few straightforward actions for each of these prompts. You may ask one employee to start speaking up and sharing their ideas in a meeting, and stop being critical if they don't voice their concerns during the production process. You might compliment them on their creative design ideas and their efforts in mentoring employees. Let your employee know that you appreciate these efforts—and that you'd love for them to continue doing these specifics.

There are several things you can do to make your feedback even more powerful and productive.

Try to understand the emotions the feedback recipient may be feeling

In a straightforward and honest way, explain the reason for the feedback. Imagine that you're giving yourself the feedback: How would *you* want to hear it? Make sure to focus on the future: What can your employee do to move forward?

Pay attention to your facial expressions when you deliver feedback

How you say things is just as important as what you're saying. Researcher Marie Dasborough studied the effects of delivery on feedback when she observed two groups: one whose members received negative feedback accompanied by positive emotional signals, such as nods and smiles, and one whose members received positive feedback delivered with frowns and narrowed eyes. People who received positive feedback accompanied by negative emotional signals reported feeling worse about their performance than participants who received good-natured negative feedback. The *delivery* of feedback can often be more important than the message itself.

How do you know whether your delivery is having a positive effect or you're provoking resentment, defensiveness, and ill will? Most of us have blind spots. Tone of voice, for example, is particularly difficult for us to detect accurately. Our facial expressions are another source of blind spots. We may feel ourselves smile, but we often don't sense other facial movements, such as our eyebrows shooting up in shock, fear, or disgust. As you feel judgment, anger, or frustration racing in, are you really able to hide it?

Another blind spot stems from the gap that exists between the intent and impact of our actions. Let's say that you gave your direct report some critical developmental feedback because you thought it was exactly what she needed to improve. You want to groom her for a promotion and career success. Yet she felt like you belittled her—in front of the whole team. As Douglas Stone and Sheila Heen point out in *Thanks for the Feedback*, we judge ourselves by our intentions, while others judge us by the effects of our actions. Trying doesn't count for much. If we fare poorly in how we execute delivering feedback, others count it against us.

How deeply do you understand your ability to give feedback well? To gain self-awareness, solicit others' help using the following strategies.

Ask for focused feedback

Ask 10 or more people—including coworkers, friends, and family—how good you are at giving feedback. Ask for specific details and examples. What was the context, what happened, and what did you do to make others respond positively to your (negative or positive) feedback? Look closely for recurring commonalities. Ideally, you'll home in on a couple of specific areas for improvement. Then use leadership coach Marshall Goldsmith's "feed forward" process, which involves five steps:

1. Describe your goal clearly. Explain that you want to provide critical feedback better. You don't want to offend people or have them become defensive. You have heard repeatedly that you are abrasive and your feedback stings.

2. Ask for suggestions. Encourage creativity. How can you connect better with employees generally, such that they feel that you care about them and their development? Employees may be less defensive when you give them critical feedback. Ask if they notice anything in particular that is responsible for you being perceived as abrasive. What specifically do they recommend that you do differently?

3. Listen carefully.

4. Thank the person. Tell the person that you appreciate them taking the time to help you and to offer specific suggestions. You might mention

that you are going to check in to see how you're progressing. Don't make excuses or get defensive.

5. Repeat this process with additional people.

If you use this approach, you'll wind up with concrete suggestions from a number of people invested in your success. Check in periodically with these people, because they can help you gauge your improvement over time.

Work with a coach

Coaches can uncover weaknesses by independently surveying and interviewing your colleagues and by shadowing you at meetings and events. A great coach can detect subtleties in your behavior of which you might not be aware and can identify underlying assumptions, experiences, and personal qualities that make you prone to being uncivil or delivering feedback poorly. What are you doing that shuts people down, closes them off to your feedback, or creates resentment?

Use colleagues or friends as coaches

Not everyone has access to coaches, but you can also reach out to colleagues and peers for help. I have personally had MBAs and executives coach one another, which has been a very effective and cost-efficient way to improve giving and receiving feedback.

While you're working to improve your own feedback (and interpersonal) skills, encourage your team members to do the same. Have an open discussion with your team about what you and your teammates do or say that conveys respect and is effective when providing feedback. What could you do or say better? Discuss what the team will gain by providing greater feedback and by delivering it with greater respect and tact. When I've done this group exercise in the past, I've found that colleagues will often spontaneously coach one another and offer candid feedback, such as: "You need to share the credit more often" or "You'd be more effective if you were more direct." It's one of the best ways to get honest, direct feedback that can move your entire team forward.

Providing effective feedback is a crucial managerial skill. Highlight the progress your team is making. Researchers Teresa Amabile and Steven Kramer have shown that a sense of progress is the most powerful motivator in the workplace, even stronger than personal recognition or pay. Encourage people's strengths by providing your employees with specific feedback on how they are helping your team or organization. Focus on *how* you deliver the feedback. Home in on potential blind spots that could be limiting the power of your feedback—or, worse, having a detrimental effect on employees. And gather feedback from others. By providing effective feedback well, you can ignite your employees, helping them and your organization thrive.

Christine Porath is a professor of management at Georgetown University and the author of *Mastering Community: The Surprising Ways We Move from Surviving to Thriving Together* (forthcoming, 2022) and *Mastering Civility: A Manifesto for the Workplace.*

NOTES

1. Gretchen Spreitzer and Christine Porath, "Creating Sustainable Performance," *Harvard Business Review*, January–February 2012.

2. Marcial Losada and Emily Heaphy, "The Role of Positivity and Connectivity in the Performance of Business Teams: A Nonlinear Dynamics Model," *American Behavioral Scientist* 47, no. 6 (2004): 740–765.

CHAPTER 10

The Right Way to Hold People Accountable

by Peter Bregman

John* was doing his best to be calm, but his frustration was palpable. Jeanine was explaining that there was little chance her group was going to make the numbers for this quarter. "Honestly?" she said. "The numbers weren't realistic to begin with. It was really unlikely that we were going to make them."

That's when John lost it. "You agreed to the numbers in our budget meeting! You came up with them!"

Jeanine was silent for a while. Then she stammered out a weak defense that John promptly tore apart. Later,

---

Adapted from content posted on hbr.org, January 11, 2016 (product #H02LQR).

when John and I were debriefing the conversation, he asked me a question that I have heard countless times from countless leaders: "How do I get my people to be more accountable for results?"

Accountability is not simply taking the blame when something goes wrong. It's not a confession. Accountability is about delivering on a commitment. It's responsibility to an outcome, not just a set of tasks. It's taking initiative with thoughtful, strategic follow-through.

And it's necessary at all levels of the hierarchy. Executives high on the org chart can't really be accountable unless the people who report to them also follow through on their commitments. This is a struggle, of course. I have seen leaders direct, question, and plead. I have seen them yell, act passive-aggressively, and throw up their hands in frustration—all in the service of "holding people accountable."

None of that works. Getting angry with people when they fall short is not a productive process for holding people accountable. It almost always reduces motivation and performance.

So what can we do to foster accountability in the people around us? We need to aim for clarity in five areas.

Clear expectations

The first step is to be crystal clear about what you expect. This means being clear about the outcome you're looking for, how you'll measure success, and how people should go about achieving the objective. It doesn't all have to come from you. In fact, the more skilled your people are, the more ideas and strategies should be coming from them. Have a genuinely two-way conversation, and before it's over, ask the other person to summarize the important pieces—the outcome they're going for, how they are going to achieve it, and how they'll know whether they're successful—to make sure you're ending up on the same page. Writing out a summary is a good idea but doesn't replace saying it out loud.

Clear capability

What skills does the person need to meet the expectations? What resources will they need? If the person does not have what's necessary, can they acquire what's missing? If so, what's the plan? If not, you'll need to delegate to someone else. Otherwise you're setting them up for failure.

Clear measurement

Nothing frustrates leaders more than being surprised by failure. Sometimes this surprise is because the person who should be delivering is afraid to ask for help. Sometimes it comes from premature optimism on both sides. Either way, it's completely avoidable. During the expectations conversation, you should agree on weekly milestones with clear, measurable, objective targets. If any of these targets slip, jump on it immediately. Brainstorm a solution, identify a fix, redesign the schedule, or respond in some other way that gets the person back on track.

Clear feedback

Honest, open, ongoing feedback is critical. People should know where they stand. If you have clear expectations, capability, and measurement, the feedback can be fact-based and easy to deliver. Is the person delivering on her commitments? Is she working well with the other stakeholders? If she needs to increase her capability, is she on track? The feedback can also go both ways—is there something you can be doing to be more helpful? Give feedback weekly, and remember it's more important to be helpful than nice.

Clear consequences

If you've been clear in all of the above ways, you can be reasonably sure that you did what's necessary to support their performance. At this point, you have three choices: repeat, reward, or release. Repeat the steps above if you feel that there is still a lack of clarity in the system. If the person succeeded, you should reward them appropriately (acknowledgment, promotion, etc.). If they have not proven accountable and you are reasonably certain that you followed the previous steps, then they are not a good fit for the role, and you should release them from it (change roles, fire them, etc.).

These are the building blocks for a culture of accountability. The magic is in the way they work together as a system. If you miss any one, accountability will fall through that gap.

I've found that it's useful to make this list public and to discuss it with the people you're asking to be accountable before there's a specific project on the line.

When I explained all of this to John, it was easy for him to identify the gaps in his communication with Jeanine. His expectations were clear, but her capability was lacking, which they had never addressed. Once they'd spoken about the gap, he could support her development with coaching while also reviewing her milestones more frequently. That gave him the data he needed to give her clear and timely feedback.

Remember the question we started with, the one that plagues so many leaders: "How do I get my people to be more accountable for results?"

Now there's an answer: It depends. Which of the five areas have you neglected?

Names have been changed.

Peter Bregman is the CEO of Bregman Partners and is recognized as the number one executive coach by Leading Global Coaches. He heads the Bregman Leadership Coach Training and the Bregman Leadership Intensive, ranked the number one leadership development program by Global Gurus. He is the bestselling author of five books, including *Leading with Emotional Courage* and *18 Minutes*, a *Wall Street Journal* bestseller.

CHAPTER 11

You Can't Be a Great Manager If You're Not a Good Coach

by Monique Valcour

Strangely, at most companies, coaching isn't part of what managers are formally expected to do. Even though research makes it clear that employees and job candidates alike value learning and career development above most other aspects of a job, many managers don't see it as an important part of their role. Yet 70% of employee learning and development happens on the job, not through

---

Adapted from content posted on hbr.org, July 17, 2014 (product #H00WOP).

formal training programs. If line managers aren't supportive and actively involved, employee growth is stunted. So is engagement and retention.

Starting today, you can be significantly more effective as a manager—and enjoy your job more—by engaging in regular coaching conversations with your team members. As you resolve to support their ongoing learning and development, here are five key tips to get you started.

Listen deeply

Consider what it feels like when you're trying to convey something important to a person who has many things on their mind. Contrast that familiar experience with the more luxurious and deeply validating one of communicating with someone who is completely focused on you and actively listening to what you have to say with an open mind and an open heart. You can open a coaching conversation with a question such as "How would you like to grow this month?" Your choice of words is less important than your intention to clear your mind, listen with your full attention, and create a high-quality connection that invites your team member to open up and to think creatively.

Ask, don't tell

As a manager, you have a high level of expertise that you're used to sharing, often in a directive manner. This is fine when you're clarifying action steps for a project you're leading or when people come to you asking for advice. But in a coaching conversation, it's essential to restrain your impulse to provide the answers. Your path is not your employee's path. Open-ended questions, not answers, are the tools of coaching. You succeed as a coach by helping your team members articulate their goals and challenges and find their own answers. This is how people clarify their priorities and devise strategies that resonate with what they care about most and that they will be committed to putting into action.

Create and sustain a developmental alliance

While your role as a coach is not to provide answers, supporting your team members' developmental goals and strategies is essential. Let's say that your employee mentions she'd like to develop a deeper understanding of how your end users experience the services your firm provides. In order to do so, she suggests accompanying an implementation team on a site visit next week, interviewing end users, and using the interviews to write an article on end-user experience for publication on your firm's intranet-based blog. You agree that this would be valuable for both the employee and the firm. Now, make sure that you give your employee the authorization, space, and resources necessary to carry out her developmental plan. In addition to supporting her, you can also highlight her article as an example of employee-directed learning and development. Follow-up is critical to build trust and to make your coaching more effective. The more you follow through on supporting your employees' developmental plans, the more productive your coaching becomes, the greater your employees' trust in you, and the more engaged you all become. It's a virtuous cycle.

Focus on moving forward positively

Oftentimes in a coaching conversation, the person you're coaching will get caught up in detailing their frustrations: "I'd love to spend more time building my network, but I have no bandwidth. I'm at full capacity just trying to stay on task with my deliverables. I'd really love to get out to some industry seminars, but I can't let myself think about it until I can get ahead of these deadlines." While it can provide temporary relief to vent, it doesn't generate solutions. Take a moment to acknowledge your employee's frustrations, but then encourage her to think about how to move past them. You might ask, "Which of the activities you mention offer the greatest potential for building your knowledge and adding value to the company?" "Could you schedule two hours of time for developmental activities each week as a recurring appointment?" "Are there skills or relationships that would increase your ability to meet your primary deliverables?" "How could we work more efficiently within the team to free up and protect time for development?"

Build accountability

In addition to making sure you follow through on any commitments you make to employees in coaching conversations, it's also useful to build accountability for the employee's side of formulating and implementing developmental plans. Accountability increases the positive impact of coaching conversations and solidifies their rightful place as keys to organizational effectiveness. If your employee plans to research training programs that will fit his developmental goals, give these plans more weight by asking him to identify appropriate programs along with their costs and the amount of time he'll need away from work, and to deliver this information to you by a certain deadline. (And then, of course, you will need to act on the information in a timely manner.)

What will coaching your employees do for you? It will build stronger bonds between you and your team members, support them in taking ownership over their own learning, and help them develop the skills they need to perform and reach their peak. And it also feels good. At a coaching workshop I led in Shanghai, an executive said the coaching exercise he'd just participated in "felt like a bungee jump." As the workshop leader, I was delighted to observe that this man, who had arrived looking reserved and a bit tired, couldn't stop smiling for the rest of the evening. He was far from the only participant who was visibly energized by the coaching experience.

So go ahead and take the interpersonal jump. You will love the thrill of coaching conversations that catalyze your employees' growth.

Monique Valcour is an executive coach, keynote speaker, and management professor. She helps clients create and sustain fulfilling and high-performance jobs, careers, workplaces, and lives. Follow her on Twitter @moniquevalcour.

CHAPTER 12

Four Reasons Good Employees Lose Their Motivation

by Richard E. Clark and Bror Saxberg

Motivation—the willingness to get the job done by start-ing rather than procrastinating, persisting in the face of distractions, and investing enough mental effort to suc-ceed—accounts for 40% of the success of team projects.[1] Yet managers are often at a loss as to how to effectively motivate uninspired employees.

Our review of research on motivation indicates that the key is for managers to first accurately identify the reason for an employee's lack of motivation and then

Adapted from content posted on hbr.org, March 13, 2019 (product #H04UA7).

apply a targeted strategy.[2] Carefully assessing the nature of the motivational failure—*before* taking action—is crucial. Applying the wrong strategy (say, urging an employee to work harder, when the reason is that they're convinced they can't do it) can actually backfire, causing motivation to falter further.

These reasons fall into a quartet of categories that we call the *motivation traps*. Here are the four traps, their distinct causes, and strategies to release an employee from their clutches.

Trap 1, Values Mismatch: *I don't care enough to do this*

How this trap ensnares employees

When a task doesn't connect with or contribute to something workers value, they won't be motivated to do it.

How to help an employee out of this trap

Find out what the employee cares about and connect it to the task. Too often, managers think about what motivates themselves and assume the same is true of their employees. Engage in probing conversation and perspective-taking to identify what your employee cares about and how that value links with the task.

There are different types of value that you can draw out. One is *interest* value, or how intellectually compelling a task is. For this, find connections between the task and the things that the employee finds intrinsically interesting. Another is *identity* value, or how central the skill set demanded by a task is to an employee's self-conception. Point out how the job at hand draws on a capacity that they consider an important part of their identity or role—such as engaging in teamwork, analytical problem solving, or working under pressure.

Importance value is how important a task is. Identify ways to highlight how crucial the task is to achieve the team's or company's mission. Finally, *utility* value is a measure of the cost of achieving (and avoiding) the task versus the larger benefits of achieving. Find ways to show how completing this particular task contributes to the employee's larger goals and avoids blowback. Sometimes it may be necessary to ask an employee to, essentially, hold their nose while carrying out an undesirable task—making clear to them the future benefit its completion will yield or the problems it will prevent.

When an employee doesn't value a task at the outset and the values mismatch may not be apparent, a manager's best bet is to try to appeal to multiple values. One or more of them may resonate with the employee.

Trap 2, Lack of Self-Efficacy: *I don't think I'm able to do this*

How this trap ensnares employees

When workers believe they lack the capacity to carry out a task, they won't be motivated to do it.[3]

How to help an employee out of this trap

Build the employee's sense of confidence and competence. This can be done in several ways. One is to point out times in the past when they've surmounted similar challenges. Perhaps share examples of others just like them who overcame the same challenges in a way the employee can do, too. Build their sense of self-efficacy with progressively more difficult challenges, or by breaking down the current task into manageable chunks.

Often, employees who lack self-efficacy are convinced that succeeding at a particular task will require the investment of far more time and energy than they can afford. Explain that they have the ability to succeed but may have misjudged the effort required; urge them to invest more effort while expressing confidence that additional effort will lead to success. It helps if managers offer some extra support as work gets underway.

Occasionally employees have the opposite motivation trap. They may lack motivation because they feel, in a sense, overqualified. Employees with inflated self-efficacy pose one of the more difficult motivational management challenges. Overconfident people often make mistakes, even as they're certain they know what they are doing. When they err, they insist that it's the *criteria* for judging success on the task that is flawed, so they take no responsibility for their failures.

When dealing with such employees, it's important to avoid challenging their ability or expertise. Instead, demonstrate to them that they have misjudged the requirements of the task, and convince them that it requires a different approach.

Trap 3, Disruptive Emotions: *I'm too upset to do this*

How this trap ensnares employees

When workers are consumed with negative emotions such as anxiety, anger, or depression, they won't be motivated to carry out a task.

How to help an employee out of this trap

Begin in a setting where you cannot be overheard. Tell them you want to understand why they are upset, and engage in active listening. Do not agree or disagree. Be nonjudgmental by asking what the employee believes is causing them to be upset. Then, briefly summarize what they said back to them and ask if you have understood. If they say no, apologize and tell them you are listening carefully and to "please try again." When people feel they have been understood, their negative emotions soften a bit. It may be useful to tell them that you want to consider what they told you and schedule a time the next day to discuss. This often helps the person get more control over their emotions.

Keep in mind that anger is the belief that someone or something external to the person has caused or will cause them harm. Ask an employee feeling angry to try to reframe their belief about the external as resulting from ignorance or accident, not intention. Suggest ways they could invest the effort to eliminate the threat. Depression sometimes results from employees' belief that they are internally inadequate in some way that they cannot control. In this case, it often helps to suggest that they are not "broken" or "inadequate" but only need to invest more effort in effective strategies. Offer your help. Anxious or fearful employees often respond positively to assistance with their approach to the task as well as to reminders that they are capable and can succeed with more effort.

If the emotions do not soften with time and effort or if they spring from outside the workplace, for example, it may be advisable to help the employee access counseling.

Trap 4, Attribution Errors: *I don't know what went wrong with this*

How this trap ensnares employees

When employees can't accurately identify the reason for their struggles with a task, or when they attribute their struggles to a reason beyond their control, they won't be motivated to do it.

How to help an employee out of this trap

Help the employee think clearly about the cause of their struggles with a task. Attribution errors are often to blame when employees seem to be finding excuses not to carry out a task (calling in sick, pleading over-commitment or "not enough time," trying to foist the task on colleagues). Helping the employee identify exactly why the task seems insurmountable can help them move past such avoidance. If they identify a cause that's out of their control (blaming other people, for example, or a flaw in themselves that can't be fixed), suggest other causes that are under their control, such as the need to adopt a new strategy or to apply a greater level of planning.

With each of these four motivation traps, the trick is to think more comprehensively about what stops employees from initiating, persisting, and putting in mental effort. The research suggests that managers can do more to diagnose the motivation problems of employees. When motivation goes off the rails, identifying exactly which trap has ensnared your employees—and applying just the right targeted intervention—can get things moving again.

———

Richard E. Clark is a professor emeritus of psychology and technology at the University of Southern California, where he is the codirector of the Center for Cognitive Technology. He's also the founding CEO of Atlantic Training, Inc., in Los Angeles.

Bror Saxberg is the vice president of learning science at the Chan Zuckerberg Initiative. He was previously the chief learning officer at Kaplan, Inc.

NOTES

1. Steven J. Condly, Richard E. Clark, and Harold D. Stolovitch, "The Effects of Incentives on Workplace Performance: A Meta-analytic Review of Research Studies," *Performance Improvement Quarterly* 16, no. 3 (2008): 46–63.

2. Richard E. Clark and Bror Saxberg, "Engineering Motivation Using the Belief-Expectancy-Control Framework," *Interdisciplinary Education and Psychology* 2, no. 1 (2018).

3. Albert Bandura, "Self-Efficacy," in *Encyclopedia of Human Behavior*, vol. 4, ed. V. S. Ramachaudran (New York: Academic Press, 1998), 71–81.

CHAPTER 13

Get Honest, Productive Feedback

by Jennifer Porter

The feedback many leaders receive is not helpful. It's often infrequent, vague, or unrelated to specific behaviors, and as a result, leaders tend to be less proactive about getting more of it. Low-quality feedback is not useful, positive feedback is undervalued, and negative feedback delivered unskillfully can actually cause physical pain.[1]

Without clear performance targets and data measuring how close or far they are from reaching them, leaders will continue to find it difficult to grow and improve.

Adapted from "How Leaders Can Get Honest, Productive Feedback," on hbr.org, January 8, 2019 (product #H04QE5).

When delivered thoughtfully, however, feedback can provide leaders with the actionable data they need to become more effective.

If you want to get the feedback that is necessary to improve your leadership, there are a few steps you can take.

Build and maintain a psychologically safe environment

Sharing feedback is often interpersonally risky. To increase the likelihood of your colleagues taking that risk with you, show them that their honesty won't be met with negative repercussions. You can do this before you ask for feedback by being curious, rewarding candor, and showing vulnerability. Being curious starts with believing that you have something useful to learn. Demonstrate that by asking your teammates open-ended questions that you really don't know the answers to: "What could go wrong if we try this?" When you listen to and genuinely explore your colleagues' different, and possibly risky, perspectives—even if you disagree with them—you are rewarding their candor. Acknowledging your weaknesses or mistakes along the way is a great way to be open and vulnerable. (For more on psychological safety, see chapter 6.)

Request both positive and negative data

Clients tell me all the time that they just want to hear "the bad stuff" when it comes to feedback. What they fail to appreciate is that positive feedback that targets a specific behavior is useful. It tells them what they *don't* need to work on and increases their motivation to focus on the behaviors that they do. For clarity, positive feedback is not the same as praise. Praise tells us someone is happy with us and thinks we are performing well. Praise sounds like: "Nice job!"; "You were great in that meeting"; "Killer presentation!" While it feels good, praise does not give us enough information to understand what we are doing effectively so that we can repeat the behavior.

When receiving feedback, give your full attention and listen carefully

Eliminate distractions, including your phone and laptop, and focus fully on the person giving the feedback. Having your phone present, even if you're not looking at it, negatively impacts relationships and reduces your ability to connect with others. Listen carefully to what the other person is saying, resisting the impulse to evaluate the accuracy of the message.

Don't debate or defend

If you find yourself disagreeing with some feedback, practice self-awareness and notice this reaction, but do not offer contradictory evidence or challenge your colleague. If you debate, you will look defensive and not open to feedback, and you may decrease the likelihood of that person offering you feedback in the future. None of these are the outcomes you're trying to achieve, so don't do it.

Own your reactions

You may feel happy, angry, confused, or frustrated by what you hear. Recognize that your reactions are about you, and not the other person. If you asked for feedback and someone was brave enough and generous enough to share it with you, it's your responsibility to own and explore your reactions. Instead of finding fault in the messenger, become curious about yourself. Ask: Where is this anger really coming from? What about this is confusing? What part of the message is actually true for me, even if I don't want to acknowledge it?

Demonstrate gratitude

Say thank you in a way that conveys sincere appreciation. If you've heard something helpful, the person giving you feedback likely spent a good amount of time considering your performance and how to thoughtfully discuss it with you. They took a risk by being candid, so let them know how much you appreciate their effort and courage.

Reflect and evaluate

Now that you have some new data, reflect on what you've heard even if you don't like reflection. By thinking through the meaning and implication of the feedback, you can learn from it and consider what parts to work on, what parts to disregard, and what parts require deeper understanding. To do this, it helps to think about your development areas, the value you place on this individual's perspective, and, possibly, what you have heard from others as well. This is also the time to come back to what you may disagree with. Given that your objective was to learn others' perspectives on you, ask yourself if it's really worth the potential damage to go back and "correct" the information. Typically, it's not.

Make a plan and take action

All of the steps before this set you up to make a plan and put it into practice. Pick one or two capabilities you want to improve, get really clear about what "improved" looks like, and then consider the steps necessary for you to learn and adopt that new behavior. Making a plan and taking action are not only important for your learning and development, they're also a signal to those who shared the feedback—you are serious about improving and you value their perspectives.

Sustain progress and share updates

You need to repeat new behaviors for at least two months for them to become new habits.[2] If you go back to your feedback providers and tell them what you are doing differently, you'll give them a catalyst to change their perspectives, validation that you heard and appreciated what they had to say, and the opportunity to see you as a person who is committed to your professional development.

Great leaders are great learners. Their never-ending pursuit of information pushes them to constantly improve and sets them apart from the rest. Getting and learning from feedback isn't always easy, but it is necessary if we want to become better. It's rare that our colleagues will offer us the kind of feedback we need to develop, and also rare that we respond in a way that rewards their efforts and helps us improve. It's worth building the skills to do this well if we want to reach our full potential.

———————————

Jennifer Porter is the managing partner of The Boda Group, a leadership and team development firm. She is an experienced operations executive and an executive and team coach.

NOTES

1. Nicole F. Roberts, "Rejection and Physical Pain Are the Same to Your Brain," *Forbes*, December 25, 2015, https://www.forbes.com/sites/nicolefisher/2015/12/25/rejection-and-physical-pain-are-the-same-to-your-brain/#7f72dd0b4f87.

2. "How Long to Form a Habit," *Psyblog*, September 2009, https://www.spring.org.uk/2009/09/how-long-to-form-a-habit.php.

Manage Everyone Effectively

CHAPTER 14

How to Retain and Engage Your B Players

by Liz Kislik

We've heard for decades that we should only hire A players and should even try to cut non–A players from our teams. But not only do the criteria for being an A player vary significantly by company, it's unrealistic to think you can work only with A players. Further, as demonstrated by Google's Aristotle project, a study of what makes teams effective, this preference for A players ignores the deep value that the people you may think of as B players actually provide.

Adapted from content posted on hbr.org, September 19, 2018 (product #H04JJF).

As I've seen in companies of all sizes and industries, stars often struggle to adapt to the culture and may not collaborate well with colleagues. B players, on the other hand, are often less concerned about their personal trajectories and are more likely to go above and beyond in order to support customers, colleagues, and the reputation of the business. For example, when one of my clients went through a disastrous changeover from one enterprise resource planning system to another, it was someone perceived as a B player who kept all areas of the business informed as she took personal responsibility for ensuring that every transaction and customer communication was corrected.

How can you support your B players to be their best and contribute the most possible, rather than wishing they were A players? Consider these five approaches to stop underestimating your B players and help them to reach their potential.

Get to know and appreciate them as the unique individuals they are

This is the first step to drawing out their hidden strengths and skills. Learn about their personal concerns, preferences, and the way they see and go about their work. Be sure you're not ignoring them because they're introverts, remote workers, or don't know how to be squeaky wheels. A senior leader I worked with had such a strong preference for extroverts that she ignored or downgraded team members who were just going about their business.

Meanwhile, the stars on her team got plenty of attention and resources, even though they often created drama and turmoil, rather than carrying their full share of responsibility for outcomes. Some of the team members she thought of as B players started turning over after long-term frustration. When the leader and some of her stars eventually left the company, some of the Bs came back and were able to make significant contributions because they supported the mission and understood the work processes.

Reassess job fit

Employees rarely do their best if they're in jobs that highlight their weaknesses rather than their strengths. They may have technical experience but no interest, or they could be weak managers but strong individual contributors. One leader I know had been growing increasingly frustrated and less effective; the pressures of satisfying the conflicting demands of different departments were too much for her. Then she took a lateral move to manage a smaller, more cohesive team focused on developing new products, and was able to focus and be inspirational again once she was freed from the pressures of managing projects in such a political environment.

Consider the possibility of bias in your assignments

Women and people of color are often overlooked for challenging or high-status assignments. They're assumed "not to be ready," or they're not considered because they don't act like commonly held but stereotyped views of "leaders." When a midlevel leader who was trying to get more exposure and advancement for one of his team members couldn't figure out what was holding her back in the eyes of the senior leader, I raised this possibility, and we strategized multiple ways that her boss could showcase the quality and impact of her work in upcoming meetings. (For more on how to spot and counteract bias, see chapter 19.)

Intentionally support them to be their best

Some people are their own worst critics or have deep-seated limiting beliefs that hold them back. When one of my clients lost a senior leader and couldn't afford to replace her at market rates, a longtime B player near the end of his career nervously filled the gap. Although he expanded his duties and kept the team going, he emphasized to both his management and himself that he wasn't really up to the job, and most of the executive team continued to treat him that way. It was not till after he had retired, and a new senior leader had to fill his shoes, that it became clear how much he had done on the organization's behalf. The executive team never came to grips with how much more he could have accomplished had they provided the relevant development, support, and appreciation all along.

Give permission to take the lead

In 30 years of practice, one of the most common reasons I've seen people hold back is they don't believe they've been given permission to step up. (The people we think of as As tend not to ask for or wait for permission.) Some B players aren't comfortable in the spotlight, but they thrive when they're encouraged to complete a mission or to contribute for the good of the company. A midlevel leader I coach is quiet, modest, and doesn't like to make waves. She kept waiting for her new leader to lay out a vision for the future and to provide direction about how the work should be done. I asked what she would do if she was suddenly in charge. She laid out a cogent plan, and I encouraged her to present it to the new leader and ask for permission to proceed. Now she and the senior leader are moving forward in partnership.

We can't all be A players, and it's unrealistic to think we'll only ever work with A players. But that may not be the appropriate goal. Instead, try using these strategies to help employees give their best, and you'll be ensuring that your whole team can turn in an A+ performance.

———————

Liz Kislik helps organizations from the *Fortune* 500 to national nonprofits and family-run businesses solve their thorniest problems. She has taught at NYU and Hofstra University, and gave a popular TEDx talk, "Why There's So Much Conflict at Work and What You Can Do to Fix It." You can receive her free guide, *How to Resolve Interpersonal Conflicts in the Workplace*, at lizkislik.com/resolve-conflict.

CHAPTER 15

Managing Your Star Employee

by Rebecca Knight

Managing your star performers should be no sweat, right? After all, they're delivering results and exceeding targets. But don't think you can just get out of their way and let them excel. They require just as much attention as everyone else. How do you manage someone who is knocking it out of the park? How do you keep stars excited about their work? And what risks should you watch out for?

What the Experts Say

Having a supremely talented employee on your team is a boss's dream. But it can be a real challenge, too,

---

Adapted from "How to Manage Your Star Employee," on hbr.org, June 30, 2017 (product #H03RC0).

according to Linda Hill, professor at Harvard Business School. You need to make sure your star has enough on her plate to stay fully engaged—but not so much that she gets burned out. And you need to offer positive feedback—but not in ways that are counterproductive to the person's growth and development. Group dynamics are another concern when you have a standout performer on your team, says Mary Shapiro, who teaches organizational behavior at Simmons University and wrote the *HBR Guide to Leading Teams*. "Real resentment can build, due to the perception that the boss is favoring the rock star," she says. Whether your star performer has just joined your team or has been working for you for a while, here are some tips on how to manage her.

Think about development

One of the hardest things about managing a supremely competent and confident employee is making sure he's sufficiently challenged in the job. The antidote to this problem is "classic talent development," Shapiro says. First, "ask your employee, 'Where do you want to go next, and what experiences do I need to give you to make sure you get there?'" Then, find opportunities to help the person acquire new skills and sharpen old ones. Hill recommends that you help the employee get "exposure to other parts of the organization" that will "broaden his perspective." And, of course, "don't neglect the B players," Hill adds. Otherwise, you're not building the capacity of the team, and "over time, people become de-skilled." Everyone on your team "deserves to be developed."

Offer autonomy

Another way to ensure your star employee stays engaged and excited about coming to work is to "give her more autonomy," Shapiro says. "Demonstrate trust by delegating authority and responsibility" over certain projects and tasks. And don't micromanage. "Give her discretion in how she does the work." If a formal promotion is not possible, or your employee is not quite ready for one, think creatively about ways to sharpen her leadership skills. "Give her training responsibilities," she adds. "Ask your rock star to work with other people on the team to mentor them and develop them."

Don't go overboard with positive feedback

Generally speaking, "stars tend to be very needy" and require more praise and reassurance than your average employee, Hill says. But you don't want to "get into the habit of feeding an ego." She recommends giving your stars "the appropriate amount of feedback" by "acknowledging their contributions." If your star executed a project beautifully or made a stellar presentation, say so. But you needn't go overboard. "Help him learn to monitor himself," she says, "and to acknowledge the contributions of other members of the team who are helping him be successful." Shapiro agrees, noting that some stars don't expect or want constant praise. "Don't assume you know what motivates them."

Manage your star's workload—and everybody else's

An important part of your job as a boss is making sure the work is divided fairly. This can be a challenge when you're managing someone who is head and shoulders above everyone else. "You want to give [all] the tasks to the rock star, because you know the rock star will get the job done," Shapiro says. But while "it's convenient for you," overwork will lead to burnout. To keep that from happening, she recommends doing "a careful analysis of what's on [your star's] plate" to identify tasks and projects that can be removed "to make capacity for other projects." It's likely that your "rock star will be reluctant to let anything go," but you must hold firm. "Be explicit and say that you want to give her more bandwidth so that she has the brainpower, energy, and time to be at her best." And beware of team burnout, Hill says. "Superstars are known as pacesetters," she says. "It can be exciting and inspiring for other people to work with them, but often others can't keep up." You need to "make sure the workload is reasonable" for everyone.

Be mindful of group dynamics

Superstars can generate team tension. Perhaps they expect performance equal to theirs from others, or peers are jealous of their abilities and treat them differently than everyone else. You can't control others' emotions, but you do have a say in the way they act. First, and most important, "don't play favorites," Hill says. Next, talk to your team members about group dynamics and their individual behavior. Your goal is to "make sure they're treating [the star] appropriately." Shapiro agrees: "You need to have one-on-one conversations with everyone. Ask, 'What motivates you and how can I help?'"

Encourage your star to build relationships

You'll need to talk to your star, too. Many high performers have trouble developing trusting relationships, Hill says. "They're quick studies, so they don't ask questions and don't try to build bridges, mostly because they don't have to." It's your job to encourage them to network and to "help them develop their capacity to engage with others and learn the power of collaboration." Explain that "to contribute to organizations today, you need to be able to work with other people in different functions." Then "be a partner in helping the person integrate with the group." Demonstrate "how his work benefits from other points of view." And use role-play to teach him how to successfully work with peers.

Don't be selfish

No one wants to lose a superstar employee, but when you're dealing with someone who's very "competent and capable," it may be a "signal that she's ready for more than you can offer" in a particular role, Shapiro says. Don't lose her to another company, though. Consider the priorities of your entire organization and whether there's a fit for her outside of your team. Be prepared "to fight battles on two fronts," Shapiro adds. "Talk to your boss about finding your star a position in the company so that she moves up, while also making sure she's replaced" with someone who will succeed in the role. It's a "common trade-off and management dilemma," adds Hill. "But you can't hoard talent."

Case Study: Encourage your star to seek out learning opportunities

Jon Stein, the CEO and founder of Betterment, the online financial adviser, says that he's been "lucky to have a number of stars" on his team over the years.

Laura*, in particular, stands out. She joined the New York City–based company as an executive assistant five years ago. She lacked experience but "she showed a lot of promise and drive," Jon recalls. During their weekly meetings, Jon gave Laura "positive feedback on the things she had done well" but also made sure to talk about areas where she could improve. The two often discussed different ways for her to take on more. It wasn't always easy to find "new challenges for her," he says. "We would set the bar ever higher with stretch goals, and it would soon become clear she could deliver."

So Jon encouraged Laura to think about her long-term prospects, "painting multiple potential career paths" for her: One day she might manage learning and development at the company, or maybe she could lead the facilities group. He then directed her to experiences that would prepare her for each of these possible roles. "I wanted to give Laura the opportunity to try new things," he says.

At the same time, Jon coached Laura on networking. He encouraged her to "build a solid peer group of more experienced people outside of the company" to accelerate her learning. "Now, whenever she has a question, she can find an answer relatively quickly. People come to her with questions, too. She has done a lot to lead and expand her network."

Giving Laura more responsibility for various corporate functions was "gradual," Jon says. Today Laura manages a team of 15 employees and has responsibility over facilities and human resources, among other areas. "She's done a great job," Jon says.

And yet he says he is always mindful about not giving Laura special treatment. Weekly one-on-one meetings between managers and direct reports are standard practice at the company. And regular employee feedback is part of the Betterment culture. "I don't play favorites," he says. "I don't want to give her opportunities that others don't get."

Names have been changed.

Rebecca Knight is currently a senior correspondent at *Insider* covering careers and the workplace. Previously she was a freelance journalist and a lecturer at Wesleyan University. Her work has been published in the *New York Times*, *USA Today*, the *Boston Globe*, and the *Financial Times*.

CHAPTER 16

Helping an Underperformer

by Amy Gallo

As a manager, you can't accept underperformance. It's frustrating, time-consuming, and it can demoralize the other people on your team. But what do you do about an employee who isn't performing up to snuff? How do you help turn around the problematic behavior? And how long do you let it go on before you cut your losses?

What the Experts Say

Your company may have a prescribed way of handling an underperformer, but most of those recommended processes aren't that useful, says Jean-François Manzoni,

---

Adapted from "How to Help an Underperformer," on hbr.org, June 23, 2014 (product #H00VK2).

a professor of management at INSEAD and coauthor of *The Set-Up-to-Fail Syndrome: How Good Managers Cause Great People to Fail.* "When you talk to senior executives, they'll usually acknowledge that those don't work," he says. So chances are, it's up to you as the manager to figure out what to do. "When people encounter an issue with underperformance, they really are on their own," says Joseph Weintraub, a professor of management and organizational behavior at Babson College and coauthor of *The Coaching Manager: Developing Top Talent in Business.* Here's how to stage a productive intervention.

Don't ignore the problem

Unfortunately, these issues commonly go unaddressed. "Most performance problems aren't dealt with directly," says Weintraub. "More often, instead of taking action, the manager will transfer the person somewhere else or let him stay put without doing anything." This is the wrong approach. Never allow underperformance to fester on your team. It's rare that these situations resolve themselves. It'll just get worse. You'll become more and more irritated, and that's going to show and make the person uncomfortable," says Manzoni. If you have an issue, take steps toward solving it as soon as possible.

Consider what's causing the problem

Is the person a poor fit for the job? Does she lack the necessary skills? Or is she just misunderstanding expectations? There is very often a mismatch between what managers and employees think is important when it comes to performance, Weintraub explains. It's critical to consider the role you might be playing in the problem. "You may have contributed to the negative situation," says Manzoni. "After all, it's rare that it's all the subordinate's fault just as it's rare that it's all the boss's." Don't focus exclusively on what the underperformer needs to do to remedy the situation—think about what changes you can make as well.

Ask others what you might be missing

Before you act, make sure to look at the problem objectively. You might talk to the person's previous boss or someone who's worked with him or conduct a 360-degree review. When approaching other people, though, do it carefully and confidentially. Manzoni suggests you might say something like: "I'm worried that my frustration may be clouding my judgment. All I can see are the mistakes he's making. I want to make an honest effort to see what I'm missing." Look for evidence that might prove your assumptions wrong.

Talk to the underperformer

Once you've checked in with others, talk to the employee directly. Explain exactly what you're observing, how the team's work is affected, and make clear that you want to help. Manzoni suggests the conversation go something like this: "I'm seeing issues with your performance. I believe that you can do better, and I know that I may be contributing to the problem. So how do we get out of this? How do we improve?" It's important to engage the person in brainstorming solutions. "Ask them to come up with ideas," says Weintraub. Don't expect an immediate response though. The person may need time to digest your feedback and come back later with some proposals.

Confirm whether the person is coachable

You can't coach someone who doesn't agree that they need help. In the initial conversation—and throughout the intervention—it's critical that the employee acknowledge the problem. "If someone says, 'I am who I am' or implies that they're not going to change, then you've got to make a decision about whether you can live with the issue and at what cost," says Weintraub. On the other hand, if you see a willingness to change and a genuine interest in improving, chances are you can work together to turn things around.

Make a plan

Create a concrete plan for what both you and the employee are going to do differently, agreeing on measurable actions so that you can mark progress. You should also ask what resources the employee needs to accomplish those goals. You don't want her to make promises she can't meet. Then, give her time. "Everyone needs time to change and maybe learn or acquire new skills," says Weintraub.

Regularly monitor their progress

It may seem obvious, but unfortunately, many managers fail to follow up. Ask the person to check in with you regularly or set up a time and date in the future to check progress. It may be helpful to ask the employee if he has someone that he'd like you to enlist in the effort. Wein-traub suggests you ask: "Is there anyone you trust who can provide me with feedback about how well you're do-ing in making these changes?" Doing this sends a posi-tive message: "It says I want this to work, and I want you to feel comfortable; I'm not going to sneak around be-hind your back."

Respect confidentiality

Along the way, it's important to keep what's happen-ing confidential, while also letting others know you're working on the underperformance problem. Manzoni admits that this is a tricky line to toe. Don't discuss the specific details with others, he says. But you might tell them something like: "Bill and I are working together on his output and lately we've had good discussions. I need your help in being as positive and supportive as you can."

If there isn't improvement, take action

If things don't get better, change the tenor of the discus-sion. "At some point you leave coaching and get into the consequences speech. You might say, 'Let me be very clear that this is the third time this has happened, and since your behavior hasn't changed, I need to explain the consequences,'" says Weintraub. Disciplinary ac-tions, particularly letting someone go, shouldn't be taken lightly. "When you fire somebody, it not only affects that person, but also you, the firm, and everybody around you," says Manzoni.

While it may be painful to fire someone, it may be the best option for your team. "It's disheartening if you see the person next to you not performing," says Weintraub. Manzoni elaborates: "The person you're asking to leave is only one of the stakeholders. The people left behind are the more important ones . . . When people feel the process is fair, they're willing to accept a negative outcome."

Praise and reward positive change

Of course, if the person makes positive changes, say so. Make clear that you're noticing the developments and reward him accordingly. "At some point, if the nonperformer has improved, be sure to take them off the death spiral. You want a team that can make mistakes and learn from them," says Weintraub.

Amy Gallo is a contributing editor at *Harvard Business Review* and the author of the *HBR Guide to Dealing with Conflict at Work* (Harvard Business Review Press, 2017) and the forthcoming *Getting Along: How to Work with Anyone (Even Difficult People)*. She writes and speaks about workplace dynamics. Follow her on Twitter @ amyegallo.

CHAPTER 17

How to Manage Someone You Don't Like

by Amy Gallo

Everybody complains about incompetent bosses or dysfunctional coworkers, but what about irritating direct reports? What should you do if the person you manage drives you up a wall? If the behavior is a performance issue, there's a straightforward way to address what's irking you, but what do you do when it's an interpersonal issue? Is it possible to be a fair boss to someone you'd avoid eating lunch with, or must you learn to like every member of your team?

Adapted from content posted on hbr.org, August 29, 2013 (product #H00B60).

What the Experts Say

Of course, your job would be a whole lot easier if you liked everyone on your team. But that's not necessarily what's best for you, the group, or the company. "People liking each other is not a necessary component to organizational success," says Ben Dattner, an organizational psychologist and the author of *The Blame Game*. Robert Sutton, a professor of management science and engineering at Stanford University and the author of *Good Boss, Bad Boss*, agrees. According to Sutton, "There's a list of things that make you like people and there's a list of things that make a group effective, and there are very different things on those lists." It's neither possible nor even ideal to build a team composed entirely of people you'd invite to a backyard barbecue. But there are real pitfalls to disliking an employee. Consciously or unconsciously, you might mismanage him or treat him unfairly and fail to see the real benefit he can deliver to your team. Here's how to get the most out of someone you don't like.

Don't assume it's a bad thing

Sure, you may grit your teeth at her lousy jokes or wince at the way he whistles at his desk, but feeling less-than-simpatico with your direct reports might not be the worst thing. "From a performance standpoint, liking the people you manage too much is a bigger problem than liking them too little," says Sutton. The employees you gravitate toward are probably the ones who act nice, don't deliver bad news, and flatter you. But it's often those who provoke or challenge you that prompt new insights and help propel the group to success. "You need people who have different points of view and aren't afraid to argue," says Sutton. "They are the kind of people who stop the organization from doing stupid things."

Focus on you

Still, the days can feel very long when you're constantly dealing with someone you don't like. It's crucial to learn how to handle your frustration. Rather than thinking about how irritating the person is, focus on why you are reacting the way you are. "They didn't create the button; they're just pushing it," says Dattner. He suggests asking yourself the following questions:

- **Is the problem the individual or someone they remind me of?** "You can have a competent person who looks like your unkind aunt and suddenly she can do no right."

- **Am I afraid of being like this person?** If your direct report constantly interrupts people, for example, and you worry you do too, you may react more strongly.

- **Are they a member of a group that I have issues with?** This question gets into a whole host of prejudices and possible legal issues, but you need to be honest with yourself about any hidden biases you may have. "Try to unpack what this person represents to you."

"You don't have to go into therapy to figure it out, but be honest with yourself about what situations or attributes make you most irritated," Dattner says. Once you've pinpointed the triggers that might be complicating your feelings, you may be able to soften or alter your reaction. Remember: It's far easier to change your perspective than to ask someone to be a different kind of person.

Put on a good face

Everyone wants their boss to like them. Whatever your feelings for your employee, he will be highly attuned to your attitude and will presume that any disapproval or distaste has to do with his performance. The onus is on you to remain fair, impartial, and composed. "Cultivating a diplomatic poker face is important. You need to be able to come across as professional and positive," says Dattner.

Seek out the positive

No one is 100% annoying. Yet it's easy to see the best in your favorites and the worst in people who bother you. "Looking for some of the flaws of your stars and the redeeming attributes of the people you don't like can help you be more balanced," says Dattner. Search for what you like about the person. "Assume the best, focus on what they're good at and how they can help your team," says Sutton. He suggests you regularly ask: "Given their talents and their limits, what can they do that would be best for the team? Can the overachiever shoulder some additional projects? Might the slow talker's snail-paced delivery spur the whole team to reflect more before speaking?"

Keep your bias out of reviews

When someone irks you, you need to be especially vigilant about keeping your bias out of the evaluation and compensation process. Dattner recommends asking yourself: "Am I using the same standards that I use for other people?" If you find you're having trouble being fair, Sutton suggests seeking counsel from another manager who is familiar with the employee's work. Ask for frank feedback on whether your evaluation matches the outsider's. You might even ask the person to play devil's advocate, to make the case for the employee's strong points. "Leadership is mischaracterized as a solo adventure. It's much more of a team sport," says Sutton.

Spend more time together

This might sound like the last thing you want to hear, but it might help to give yourself more exposure to the problem employee. Sometimes strong medicine is the most effective cure. Sutton cites studies that demonstrate how collaboration on difficult tasks tends to build affinity. "Over time, if you work together closely, you may come to appreciate them," he says. Consider staffing him to your toughest project, or asking him to serve as your right-hand person on an important initiative. Most important, remember to keep an open mind. "Your favorite employee today might become your least favorite tomorrow. The people you like may become untrustworthy tomorrow," says Dattner.

Amy Gallo is a contributing editor at *Harvard Business Review* and the author of the *HBR Guide to Dealing with Conflict at Work* (Harvard Business Review Press, 2017) and the forthcoming *Getting Along: How to Work with Anyone (Even Difficult People)*. She writes and speaks about workplace dynamics. Follow her on Twitter @amyegallo.

Help All Employees Thrive

CHAPTER 18

Get Over Your Fear of Talking About Diversity

by Daisy Auger-Dominguez

While 27% of chief diversity officers find themselves still having to make the case for diversity, inclusion, and belonging in the workplace, the good news is that the majority of top leaders already understand how critical these efforts are.[1] Indeed, in my work in talent and diversity at Google, Disney, and other large firms, I've found many leaders eager for actionable frameworks and advice to create more inclusive cultures. But again and again I find one thing plaguing their attempts: fear.

Adapted from "Getting Over Your Fear of Talking About Diversity," on hbr.org, November 8, 2019 (product #H05949).

These leaders are so terrified about messing up and saying the wrong thing to all their stakeholders—employees, board members, funders, clients, customers—or the wider world via social media that they're paralyzed into inaction. Take my experience at Google in the summer of 2015, during the expansion of the Black Lives Matter movement. Black employees led walkouts to shine a light on the marginalization and structural inequities they faced in the workplace. Several of my white manager-level colleagues approached me to express their anxiety about how to effectively engage with their employees of color about the protests. Should they say something? Do something? How could they, as white leaders, speak about anything related to the Black experience without offending anyone? Would I look over messages they were drafting for their teams before they sent them? They needed encouragement, permission, and advice before they could do the work of inclusive leadership.

It is critical that leaders not put this work onto employees of color but rather be visible doing this work themselves. When they don't, they lose their teams' trust and belief in their willingness to lead fairly—and they also set a poor example. I've led inclusion strategy and learning discussions at startups after which founders expressed dismay that their leadership teams did not participate more actively. If you want your team to stand up for inclusion, *you* need to stand up.

Don't let fear hold you back from this full engagement. Here's what I tell leaders who are afraid of taking a misstep when trying to solve for diversity, equity, and inclusion in their workplaces.

Ask Better Questions

Genuine inquiry can promote trusting relationships and a safe, respectful, and supportive work environment even in times of complex change. And because you don't have to pretend you're more knowledgeable about these topics than you already are, asking questions can also help you overcome uncomfortable silences and awkward exchanges regarding power and privilege.

This doesn't mean tasking others with achieving your own goals: "How do we move the needle on our diversity and inclusion gaps?" Instead, seek to understand what challenges your employees face every day, especially any practices and behaviors that are causing them pain. Ask questions like:

- What are the biggest barriers to your success and what role can I play in helping to remove them?

- Do you feel safe enough to take risks at work? To contribute? To belong to the community?

- What percentage of your time is spent on addressing exclusion or microaggressions against you or others?

- Whose voice or what perspective is missing from this conversation?

- How can I help amplify your voice and that of other underrepresented voices?

If you're afraid of making a vocabulary blunder—using the wrong terminology for someone's race, for example, or misgendering people—just ask about their pronouns or what role race plays in how they experience the workplace. Most often you will find that your employees will welcome feeling seen and valued. For those who have been unduly bearing the burden of marginalization and exclusion, though, some questions may trigger deeply held emotions. In those cases, honor whether they want to engage in your questions or not. You can also offer another opportunity to speak if they don't want to do so in the moment.

Show courage not just in what you ask but in how you listen. Suspend your judgment, reduce your instinct to respond reactively, and take time to deeply reflect on what your people are telling you. Demonstrate your interest in the other person's answers, and check to make sure you're understanding them.

As a leader you need to be careful in the words you use, but don't let your fear replace your curiosity.

Read Up

There is no playbook for standing face-to-face with inequity, injustice, and oppression while running a business or organization. But there are many resources that can help you better understand the dynamics and the voices at play. Educate yourself on the issues women, people of color, people with disabilities, LGBTQ+, religious minorities, and other marginalized groups face, and the compounding effects of intersectional identities.

There are many books on these topics, and the best entry point depends in part on your own experiences. But a few go a long way. To improve your knowledge and ability to engage in racial dialogue, I suggest Ijeoma

Oluo's *So You Want to Talk About Race.* (I focus on race in these recommendations because I find that it's the most challenging topic for leaders to address—and that it's often the root cause of other abuses of power in the workplace.) To better understand the experience of women of color in the workplace in particular, see Minda Harts's *The Memo: What Women of Color Need to Know to Secure a Seat at the Table.* For an exploration of identity, gender, and race, read Jodi Patterson's *The Bold World.* And for a more general look at how to lead in an inclusive way, take up Dolly Chugh's *The Person You Mean to Be: How Good People Fight Bias.*

Lean Into the Uncomfortable

As a leader in today's world, you are grappling with complex change on many levels while trying to understand human dynamics that can feel untranslatable, conflicting, and painful. But that's OK.

The only way to address the challenges associated with racism, sexism, and other forms of injustice in the workplace is to be open to experiencing this discomfort in an honest and forthright way. Push yourself to communicate candidly about difficult topics. Accept that you are never going to be perfect. Apologize and admit your mistakes and blind spots, express gratitude when someone corrects you, listen to those who have been injured or silenced, and commit to doing better. Then pick yourself up, go out there again, and do better.

Your actions as a leader are doubly powerful. In addition to standing up for others yourself, you signal to others that it is also safe for them to do so.

Just Get Started

There are no shortcuts nor silver bullets for enabling inclusive workplaces. But you need to start somewhere. Whether it's launching team conversations about white fragility, holding all-hands meetings calling out racially charged incidents when they happen, or introducing yourself with your pronouns, you can send a powerful message as an ally in a position of power and influence when you're the one who takes up the work.

Daisy Auger-Dominguez is a global human capital executive, board member, adviser, speaker, and inclusion expert. Her mission is to make workplaces more equitable and inclusive. She is currently chief people officer at VICE Media Group. Check out her TEDx talk and forthcoming book *Inclusion Revolution*.

NOTE

1. "Paving the Way for Diversity & Inclusion Success," Weber Shandwick, September 18, 2019, https://www.webershandwick.com/news/paving-the-way-for-diversity-inclusion-success/.

CHAPTER 19

How the Best Bosses Interrupt Bias on Their Teams

by Joan C. Williams and Sky Mihaylo

Companies spend millions on antibias training each year. The goal is to create workforces that are more inclusive, and thereby more innovative and more effective. Studies show that well-managed diverse groups outperform homogeneous ones and are more committed, have higher collective intelligence, and are better at making decisions and solving problems. But research also shows

---

Adapted from an article in *Harvard Business Review*, November–December 2019 (product #R1906L).

that bias prevention programs rarely deliver. And some companies don't invest in them at all. So how can you, as an individual leader, make sure your team is including and making the most of diverse voices? Can one person fix what an entire organization can't?

Although bias itself is devilishly hard to eliminate, it is not as difficult to *interrupt*. In the decades we've spent researching and advising people on how to build and manage diverse work groups, we've identified ways that managers can counter bias without spending a lot of time—or political capital.

The first step is to understand the four distinct ways bias plays out in everyday work interactions: (1) *Prove it again*: Some groups have to prove themselves more than others do. (2) *Tightrope*: A narrower range of behaviors is accepted from some groups than from others. (3) *Maternal wall*: Women with children see their commitment and competence questioned or face disapproval for being too career focused. (4) *Tug-of-war*: Disadvantaged groups find themselves pitted against one another because of differing strategies for assimilating—or refusing to do so.

The second step is to recognize when and where these forms of bias arise day-to-day. In the absence of an organizational directive, it's easy to let them go unaddressed. That's a mistake. You can't be a great manager without becoming a *bias interrupter*. Here's how to do it.

Picking Your People

Bias in hiring has been extensively documented. In one study, "Jamal" needed eight more years of experience than "Greg" to be seen as equally qualified. Another found that men from elite backgrounds were called back for interviews more than 12 times as often as identical candidates from nonelite backgrounds. Other studies have found that women, LGBTQ+ candidates, people with disabilities, women in headscarves, and older people are less likely to be hired than their peers.

Fairness in hiring is only the first step toward achieving diversity, but it's an important one. Here are four simple actions that will yield the best candidates by eliminating artificial advantages:

1. Insist on a diverse pool

Whether you're working with recruiters or doing the hiring yourself, make it clear from the outset that you want true diversity, not just one female or minority candidate. Research shows that the odds of hiring a woman are 79 times as great if at least two women are in the finalist pool, while the odds of hiring a nonwhite candidate are 194 times as great with at least two finalist minority applicants. For example, when Kori Carew launched the Shook Scholars Institute at Shook, Hardy & Bacon, she designed it to bring a diverse mix of students into the law firm and offered career development and mentoring that prompted many of them to apply for summer associate positions.

2. Establish objective criteria, define "culture fit," and demand accountability

Implicit biases around culture fit often lead to homogeneity. Too often it comes down to shared backgrounds and interests that out-groups, especially first-generation professionals, won't have. That's why it's important to clarify objective criteria for any open role and to rate all applicants using the same rubric. When one insurance company began hiring in this way, it ended up offering jobs to 46% more minority candidates than before. Even if your organization doesn't mandate this approach, ensure that everyone on your team takes it. Write down the specific qualifications required for a particular position so that everyone can focus on them when reviewing résumés and conducting interviews. For example, when Alicia Powell was managing chief counsel at PNC Bank, she made a point of listing the qualities that would make new team members successful in their roles: proactive in managing risk, self-disciplined, patient, customer focused, and independent. Powell shared this information with the rest of her team and candidates, ensuring that everyone was on the same page. You should hold people accountable in the same way. Waive criteria rarely, and require an explanation for those exceptions; then keep track of long-term waiving trends. Research shows that objective rules tend to be applied rigorously to out-groups but leniently to in-groups.

3. Limit referral hiring

If your organization is homogeneous, hiring from within or from employees' social networks will only perpetuate that. So reach out to women and minority groups. Google partners with historically Black colleges such as Spelman and Florida A&M University and with Hispanic-serving institutions such as New Mexico State and the University of Puerto Rico, Mayagüez. As an individual leader, you can work with the same organizations or recruit from similar ones in your industry or local community.

4. Structure interviews with skills-based questions

Ask every person interviewed the same questions and make sure that each question directly relates to the desired knowledge and skills you've outlined. Rate the answers immediately—that will allow you to compare candidates fairly on a preestablished rubric and prevent favoritism. You should also use skills assessments: Rather than ask "How comfortable are you with Excel?" say "Here's a data set. How would you find out X?" For more-complex skills, such as project management, pose a problem or a task that candidates are likely to encounter on the job and ask them to describe in detail how they would handle it.

Managing Day-to-Day

Even good leaders sometimes fall into bad habits when it comes to the daily management of their teams. Women report doing about 20% more "office housework," on average, than their white male counterparts, whether it's literal housework (arranging for lunch or cleaning up after a meeting), administrative tasks (finding a place to meet or prepping a PowerPoint), emotional labor ("He's upset—can you fix it?"), or undervalued work (mentoring summer interns). This is especially true in high-status, high-stakes workplaces. Women engineers report a "worker bee" expectation at higher rates than white men do, and women of color report it at higher rates than white women do. Meanwhile, glamour work that leads to networking and promotion opportunities, such as project leadership and presentations, goes disproportionately to white men. When the consultancy GapJumpers analyzed the performance reviews of a tech company client, it found that women employees were 42% more likely than their male colleagues to be limited to lower-impact projects; as a result, far fewer of them rose to more-senior roles.

Meetings are another problem area. Research shows that men are more likely than women to dominate the conversation, and that whereas men with expertise tend to be *more* influential, women with expertise tend to be *less* so. Our study of lawyers found that half of women report being interrupted in meetings at a higher rate than their male peers are. Another study found that in meetings that included more men than women (a common scenario), women typically participated about 25% less often than their male coworkers did. Double standards and stereotypes play out whenever diverse identities come together. Is a woman "emotional," or a Black man "angry," while a white male is "passionate"? We once heard from a woman scientist that she was sharply criticized as "aggressive" when she brought up a flaw in a male colleague's analysis; after that she felt she needed to just "bring in baked goods and be agreeable." A Black tech company executive we know told us about a meeting during which she said little while the only other woman, an Asian American, said a lot. But she later heard that people thought she had "dominated" the conversation while her Asian American peer had been "very quiet."

Unsure whether this sort of thing is happening on your team? Start tracking assignments and airtime in meetings. Use our free online tools to find out which work done by your group is higher- or lower-profile and who's doing what.[1] For meetings, pay attention: Who's at the table? Who's doing the talking? Is someone taking notes when he or she could be leading the conversation? If you find a problematic dynamic, here are some ways to change it:

1. Set up a rotation for office housework, and don't ask for volunteers

"I always give these tasks to women because they do them well/volunteer" is a common refrain. This dynamic reflects an environment in which men suffer few consequences for bypassing or doing a poor job on low-value work, while women who do the same are seen as "prima donnas" or incompetent. Particularly when administrative staff is limited, a rotation helps level the playing field and makes it clear that everyone is expected to contribute to office housework. If you ask for volunteers, women and people of color will feel powerful pressure to prove they are "team players" by raising their hands.

2. Mindfully design and assign people to high-value projects

Sometimes we hear "It's true, I keep giving the plum assignments to a small group—but they're the only ones with the skills to do them!" According to Joyce Norcini, formerly general counsel for Nokia Siemens Networks, if you have only a tight circle of people you trust to handle meaningful work, you're in trouble. Her advice: Reconsider who is capable of doing what these important jobs require; chances are someone not on your usual list is. You may need to move outside your comfort zone and be more involved in the beginning, but having a broader range of trained people will serve you well in the end.

3. Acknowledge the importance of lower-profile contributions

"Diversity" hires may lag behind their majority-member peers because they're doing extra stuff that doesn't get them extra credit. If your organization truly prioritizes inclusion, then walk your talk. Many bosses who say they value diversity programming and mentorship don't actually take it into account when promotion or comp time becomes available. Integrating these contributions into individual goal setting and evaluating them during performance reviews is a simple start. And don't be afraid to think big: A law partner we know did such a great job running the women's initiative that the firm begged her to stay on for another year. She said she would if the firm's bosses made her an equity partner. They did.

4. Respond to double standards, stereotyping, "manterruption," "bropriating," and "whipeating"

Pay close attention to the way people on your team talk about their peers and how they behave in group settings. For example, men tend to interrupt women far more often than the other way around; displays of confidence and directness *decrease* women's influence but *increase* men's. If a few people are dominating the conversation in a meeting, address it directly. Create and enforce a policy for interruptions. Keep track of those who drown others out and talk with them privately about it, explaining that you think it's important to hear everyone's contributions. Similarly, when you see instances of "bropriating" or "whipeating"—that is, majority-group members taking or being given credit for ideas that women and people of color originally offered—call it out. We know two women on the board of directors of a public company who made a pact: When a man tried to claim one of their ideas, the other would say something like, "Yes, I liked Sandra's point, and I'm glad you did too." Once they did this consistently, bropriating stopped.

5. Ask people to weigh in

Women, people of Asian descent, and first-generation professionals report being brought up with a "modesty mandate" that can lead them to hold back their thoughts or speak in a tentative, deferential way. Counter this by extending an invitation: "Camilla, you have experience with this—what are we missing? Is this the best course of action?"

6. Schedule meetings inclusively

Business meetings should take place in the office, not at a golf course, a university club, or your favorite concert venue. Otherwise you're giving an artificial advantage to people who feel more comfortable in those settings or whose personal interests overlap with yours. Whenever possible, stick to working hours, or you risk putting caregivers and others with a demanding personal life at a disadvantage. Joan once noticed that no mothers were participating in a faculty appointment process because all the meetings were held at 5:30 p.m. When she pointed this out to the person leading them, the problem was fixed immediately. This colleague had a stay-at-home wife and simply hadn't thought about the issue before.

7. Equalize access proactively

Bosses may meet with some employees more regularly than others, but it's important to make sure this is driven by business demands and team needs rather than by what individuals want or expect. White men may feel more comfortable walking into your office or asking for time. The same may be true of people whose interests you share. When Emily Gould Sullivan, who has led the employment law functions for two *Fortune* 500 retail companies, realized that she was routinely accepting "walking meeting" invitations from a team member who was, like her, interested in fitness, she made a point of reaching out to others to equalize access.

Developing Your Team

Your job as a manager is not only to get the best performance out of your team but also to encourage the development of each member. That means giving fair performance reviews, equal access to high-potential assignments, and promotions and pay increases to those who have earned them. Unfortunately, as we've noted, some groups need to prove themselves more than others, and a broader range of behaviors is often accepted from white men. For example, our research shows that assertiveness and anger are less likely to be accepted from people of color, and expectations that women will be modest, self-effacing, and nice often affect performance assessments. One study found that 66% of women's reviews contained comments about their personalities, but only 1% of men's reviews did. These double standards can have a real impact on equity outcomes. PayScale found that men of color were 25% less likely than their white peers to get a raise when they asked for one. And gender norms stunt careers for women. PayScale found that when women and men start their careers on the same rung of the professional ladder, by the time they are halfway (aged 30–44), 47% of men are managers or higher, but only 40% of women are. These numbers just worsen over time: Only 3% of the women make it to the C-suite, compared with 8% of the men.

Take these steps to avoid common pitfalls in evaluations and promotions:

1. Clarify evaluation criteria and focus on performance, not potential

Don't arrive at a rating without thinking about what predetermined benchmarks you've used to get there. Any evaluation should include enough data for a third party to understand the justification for the rating. Be specific. Instead of "She writes well," say "She can write an effective summary judgment motion under a tight deadline."

2. Separate performance from potential and personality from skill sets

In-groups tend to be judged on their potential and given the benefit of the doubt, whereas out-groups have to show they've nailed it. If your company values potential, it should be assessed separately, with factors clearly outlined for evaluators and employees. Then track whether there's a pattern as to who has "potential." If so, try relying on performance alone for everyone or get even more concrete with what you're measuring. Personality comments are no different; be wary of double standards that affect women and people of color when it comes to showing emotion or being congenial. Policing women into femininity doesn't help anyone, and—as courts have pointed out—it's direct evidence of sex discrimination. If that's not motivation enough, evaluators can miss critical skills by focusing on personality. It's more valuable, and accurate, to say someone is a strong collaborator who can manage projects across multiple departments than to say "She's friendly and gets along with everyone."

3. Level the playing field with respect to self-promotion

The modesty mandate mentioned above prevents many people in out-groups from writing effective self-evaluations or defending themselves at review time. Counter that by giving everyone you manage the tools to evaluate their own performance. Be clear that it's acceptable, and even expected, to advocate for oneself. A simple two-pager can help overcome the modesty mandate and cue majority men (who tend toward overconfidence) to provide concrete evidence for their claims.

4. Explain how training, promotion, and pay decisions will be made, and follow those rules

As the chair of her firm's women's initiative, one lawyer we know developed a strategy to ensure that all candidates for promotion were considered fairly. She started with a clear outline of what was needed to advance and then assigned every eligible employee (already anonymized) to one of three groups: green (meets the objective metrics), yellow (is close), and red (doesn't). Then she presented the color-coded list to the rest of the evaluation team. By anonymizing the data and pregrouping the candidates by competencies, she ensured that no one was forgotten or recommended owing to in-group favoritism.

All the evaluators were forced to stick to the predetermined benchmarks, and as a result, they tapped the best candidates. (Those in the yellow category were given advice about how to move up to green.) When it comes to promotions, there may be limits to what you can do as an individual manager, but you should push for transparency on the criteria used. When they are explicit, it's harder to bend the rules for in-group members.

Conclusion

Organizational change is crucial, but it doesn't happen overnight. Fortunately, you can begin with all these recommendations *today*.

Joan C. Williams is a distinguished professor of law, Hastings Foundation chair, and founding director of the Center for WorkLife Law at the University of California, Hastings Law. An expert in the field of social inequality, Williams is the author of 12 books including *White Working Class: Overcoming Class Cluelessness in America* (Harvard Business Review Press, 2017) and *Bias Interrupted: Creating Inclusion for Real and for Good* (Harvard Business Review Press, 2021). She is widely known for "bias interrupters"—an evidence-based, metrics-driven approach to eradicating implicit bias in the workplace; the website www.biasinterrupters.org with open-sourced toolkits for organizations and individuals has been accessed 225,000 times in countries worldwide.

Sky Mihaylo is a candidate for a master's of public policy degree at UC Berkeley's Goldman School of Public Policy. Formerly a policy and research fellow at the Center for WorkLife Law, she now helps organizations build better teams and services through equity-minded strategic planning.

NOTE

1. Tools for Organizations, Bias Interrupters, https://biasinterrupters.org/toolkits/orgtools/.

CHAPTER 20

Managing a Hybrid Workforce

by Rebecca Knight

Your employees' needs are always varied. But as many companies embrace a mix of in-office and remote work, your team members are likely contending with vastly different situations. As the leader, how do you manage these various circumstances while treating everyone fairly? What protocols can you put in place to ensure that the employees in the office are in sync with those working from home? And how do you remain flexible when plans change?

Adapted from "How to Manage a Hybrid Team," on hbr.org, October 7, 2020 (product #H05W73).

What the Experts Say

Having a team in which some employees are co-located in an office and others are doing their jobs remotely presents a number of challenges for managers, says Liane Davey, cofounder of 3COze Inc. and author of *You First: Inspire Your Team to Grow Up, Get Along, and Get Stuff Done*. Some of these challenges might feel familiar. For instance, there could be an "us versus them" undercurrent among colleagues "similar to the phenomenon of having a head office and a satellite office," she says. There could also be the same kind of communication, team engagement, and coordination issues that are common with geographically distributed teams. Linda Hill, professor at Harvard Business School, suggests you start by asking: "What is the experience my employees are having at work, and how can I empower them to do the best they can?" Here are some tips.

Create and set expectations

Talk with your team members about creating the practices and protocols they need for hybrid work. "Consider this an opportunity to affirm the aspects of your organization's culture that you want to be the same, and talk about those that need to be adapted," says Hill. "Have an explicit discussion about how and when you're going to communicate, who has access to what information, who needs to be in which meetings, and who needs to be in on which decisions." She recommends coming to an agreement on norms for communicating—Should people always include the entire team? Must recipients acknowledge every message?—and set guidelines for when to use what channel, whether it's email, Slack, phone, etc.

Talk, too, about how employees plan to structure their working hours. "The end of the day is becoming nebulous," Hill says. "People out of the office may want flexibility and the freedom to rework their hours, and the people in the office may want more structure. Sometimes compromises will be necessary." Your goal as a group is to build and enforce a new culture by figuring out what makes for the best way to work in a hybrid environment.

Prioritize with flexibility in mind

No matter where they're working, your employees will always need some amount of flexibility to live their lives. But a doctor's appointment doesn't have to interfere with work getting done. The best way to prepare is to set clear priorities so that everyone on your "team knows what's most important," says Davey. She suggests holding a regular "Monday huddle," where you prioritize the most important work that needs to get done that week. In addition, you should discuss the deliverables that would be "nice to have if workers have discretionary time." Focusing on the most important work builds flexibility into the system. If, say, a working parent needs leeway to pick up their child from school, others can ideally pick up the slack.

Emphasize inclusion

Building a fair and equitable workplace is more complicated when you're running a hybrid team, says Hill. There's a proximity bias that leads to the incorrect

assumption that "the people in the office are more productive than those who are not," she says. As a leader, you
need to put in place practices to counteract this ten-
dency. Davey suggests establishing the basic ground
rule that all-team meetings take place over Zoom—
even though some people may be together in the office.
There's something about having "everyone's face appear
in those little *Brady Bunch* boxes that equalizes things,"
she says. What's more, hybrid meetings are unfair to
those not physically in the space. "It's hard to listen when
you're not there," she says. "There is inevitably side chat-
ter in the room, and someone is always shuffling paper."

You mustn't tolerate team members in the office talking about work in a way that even inadvertently excludes
remote colleagues, adds Hill. You need to make sure that
everyone on your team is given the opportunity to weigh
in. She suggests saying something simple like, "Let's get
Jane on the phone to discuss this."

Strive for equity

Another risk in a hybrid environment is that it will ex-
acerbate "your own baggage and biases about particular
employees," says Davey. In other words, you'll continue
to hold your star employees in high regard and you'll
"continue to see the employees you're adversely predis-
posed to in a negative light." It may be human nature,
but that doesn't make it right.

The first step is to pay attention, says Davey. Are you
inclined to give the benefit of the doubt to the employee
you think is terrific? And do you discount the needs of
the employee who annoys you? "Ask yourself, are there

people on this team that I have not given a fair shake to, and what would it look like if I did?" she says.

Next, pay attention to how you divvy up your day. "Look at who you're spending time with," says Hill. Is it people who are in the office with you? "Don't fall into easy patterns," she says. Finally, make a concerted effort to do better. Think about ways you can position all your team members for success. Make sure, too, that you're using objective data to evaluate their performance.

Watch for signs of burnout

It's critical that you pay close attention to your team members' stress levels, especially for employees you don't see every day. People do get stressed, irritable, and exhausted, of course—including you. But if you notice that someone is behaving differently—maybe "someone who was talkative and outspoken is now docile, or someone who was calm and composed now has a shorter fuse," explains Hill, consider it a sign of burnout.

Davey recommends taking steps to help your employee. For instance, if a team member tells you they're overwhelmed, try helping them prioritize. "They may have seven big things on their plate, but of those, only two things really matter," she says. "If somebody is in a bad spot, help them through it day by day; if that's too hard, go task by task," she says. "Focus and connection are the antidote to burnout."

Make it fun

It's also worth thinking about "how to bring some playfulness into the workday." Many of us miss the laughter and levity from our prepandemic lives. She suggests holding an "informal Zoom room" every day around lunchtime so that people can chat freely like they would in the office lunchroom. "Find times where there is no agenda," where people can chat about books they're reading, their kids, or their latest Netflix obsessions—making sure that these events are open to everyone on the team regardless of where they're working. You might even try themed lunches where colleagues wear colorful scarves or make different types of cuisine (or get take-out). "Have fun with it," she says. "It doesn't always have to be serious." Your aim, adds Hill, is "to make people feel connected" and to create a sense of community.

Take heart

Finally, don't expect any of this to be easy. There will be bumps along the way. Be humble. And be patient. "It's a new time," says Hill. "It requires a whole new level of being present, being agile, and being able to adapt." But look at the bright side. The rise of hybrid work, brought on by the Covid-19 pandemic, "is forcing you to develop skills and implement practices that will stand you in great stead for the rest of your career," says Davey.

Case Study: Help employees communicate, collaborate, and stay in sync

After the Canadian government gave companies the green light to reopen during the pandemic, Marc Boscher, head of Montreal-based Unito, a workflow management platform company, allowed his employees the option of returning to the office or continuing to work from home.

"Some people really wanted to get out of their house," he says. "Others didn't want to come back or couldn't for health and family reasons."

As Boscher ran a hybrid team during the crisis, his top priority was to make sure all of his 60 employees felt they were being treated fairly. "In the past, there might be a first-class-/second-class-citizen dynamic with remote workers." To maintain equality, he issued a new policy that all meetings take place online. "Everyone is on the same level," he says.

In addition, all meetings are recorded so that employees have the freedom to work asynchronously. This was critical in a pandemic that increased pressures on employees' family lives, he says.

"The person holding the meeting sends out a prepared agenda in advance so that if a colleague doesn't think they need to be there, they can opt out," he says. "You can read the summary or watch the meeting at twice the speed [and you're caught up]. It removes the pressure on employees and lets them choose when they consume the information."

Helping his team members stay on track and in sync is another priority. Teams are encouraged to leverage collaboration tools and document every change and decision that gets made. This helps everyone stay on the same page, he says.

The biggest challenge, according to Boscher, is to ensure that Unito maintains its positive culture and offers opportunities for colleagues to form strong relationships.

Because employees are working under different circumstances, "we constantly have to work on our culture."

For example, he's helped create optional outdoor team-building events. The company has hosted happy hours in parks around the city, encouraging different groups of people to show up and safely interact. Colleagues have also organized team hikes, bike rides, and walking meetings.

In addition, Boscher has allotted time in the week for employees to use a matching tool in Slack that puts colleagues from different departments together for 15- to 30-minute coffee dates. "I am trying to re-create some of the serendipity of watercooler conversations."

All in all, he says, the hybrid workplace has been a positive "chance to experiment" and try new ways of working. "It's been a good forcing mechanism, and we are proving that we're flexible and open-minded to change."

———————

Rebecca Knight is currently a senior correspondent at *Insider* covering careers and the workplace. Previously she was a freelance journalist and a lecturer at Wesleyan University. Her work has been published in the *New York Times*, *USA Today*, the *Boston Globe*, and the *Financial Times*.

CHAPTER 21

Build Trust on Your Cross-Cultural Team

by Andy Molinsky and Ernest Gundling

One of the most essential characteristics for a high-functioning team—perhaps the single most important characteristic—is trust. Anyone who has worked on a team knows that team members must be able to trust one another to get the job done, and be committed and dedicated to the overall welfare of the group. In any group of individuals, trust is challenging to create and sustain, but in the case of a multicultural team, it can be especially difficult for a variety of different reasons.

Adapted from content posted on hbr.org, June 28, 2016 (product #H02WY4).

First of all, communication styles vary across cultures; so, too, does the extent to which people socialize or get down to business at the start of a meeting. There are differences in conventions around time, giving feedback, and disagreeing publicly. Multicultural teams are prone to friction due to perceptions of ethnocentrism, with minority team members feeling ignored or not taken seriously.

How can leaders of multicultural teams leverage the upside of diversity without falling prey to its inherent challenges? In our collective experience working with hundreds of individuals on cross-cultural teams around the globe, leaders of multicultural teams can use the following five tips to build trust between team members.

Structure the team for success

The late, great organizational behavior scholar Richard Hackman used to argue that the best way to ensure a positive process in a team is to create initial conditions that set up the team for success. For a multicultural team, that means making sure the team has a clear and compelling direction, its members have access to the information and resources they need to successfully carry out the work, stakeholders in different geographies and functions are on board with the team's agenda, and the team is staffed wisely—ideally with people who have the requisite technical skills as well as cultural intelligence and global dexterity. Given the built-in challenges these teams face to begin with, it's essential to staff them with as many curious, flexible, thoughtful, and emotionally stable members as possible.

Understand the cross-cultural makeup of your team

The leader of any cross-cultural team needs to understand the different cultures, language differences, and "fault lines" within the team, as well as the potential for misconception and miscommunication. For example, if the team comprises three Germans and three Koreans, you might guess that feedback will be a cultural tripwire. Many Germans are notoriously comfortable giving direct, unmitigated feedback, whereas the reverse is typically the case in Korea unless the dialogue is between senior and junior colleagues. Making note of these tensions can help you anticipate potential challenges and resolve them swiftly and effectively.

That said, leaders also must understand individual personalities. What if the three Korean members of the team all went to school in the United States, lived and worked in Europe, and are anything but prototypical Korean in their cultural style? That would make for a very different set of predictions about group dynamics.

Set very clear norms and stick to them

Multicultural team members are inevitably going to bring a wide variety of different work styles and personal preferences to the table. The team leader must establish team norms that everyone sticks to—no matter what their personal default might be. Rather than simply imposing your own preferred style, start by taking into account what will work best for the team as a whole, and consider incorporating practices from other cultures that could be useful. For instance, if you normally assign individual responsibilities but many team members have a preference for handling work in small project groups, you could assign complex tasks to small groups.

Make the norms clear, but be aware of who on the team might find it difficult to meet those expectations due to cultural backgrounds. You may need additional communication for those team members. For example, if you have established that team members must arrive at meetings by the designated time to ensure a prompt start (Western-style punctuality), you'll need to reinforce that norm consistently across the group. The same goes for patterns of communication. Multicultural team members benefit from knowing what type of information they will receive when, and from having a regular rhythm for video conferences, teleconferences, email updates, and one-on-one discussions. This creates context and predictability that helps to compensate for those instances when team members are remote from one another. Of course, sometimes things change and adjustment is required, but in general, keeping a consistent, clear structure regarding work styles and expectations is a critical way to create a common-ground team culture.

Find ways to build personal bonds

Both of us have found that one of the most powerful tools in easing potential conflict on a team is establishing personal connections. Naturally, different global cultures have different norms about relationship building. In some cultures, like the United Kingdom, it takes a long time for people to build a friendship; in other cultures, like Brazil, it seemingly happens overnight. Given this, you may not be able to encourage deep, personal relationships, but you can foster rapport and individual connections. Perhaps you discover that someone with a completely different background from you is also an amateur photographer, or you both have children who play the piano. You'd be surprised at the power of these personal bonds, especially on a multicultural team. Leaders must create conditions for these connections to form: Organize social events, pair quieter team members with vocal ones, or directly facilitate introductions between specific members who you think might have hidden commonalities. Chances are, the benefits will circle directly back to the team.

When conflict arises, address it immediately

Conflict is inevitable in any team, let alone a multicultural one. If tension arises, address it quickly so that a small conflict doesn't balloon into something impossible to manage. Leaders need to be capable of understanding multiple cultural perspectives and serving as a cultural bridge between parties in conflict situations. This may require an understanding of indirect as well as direct communication styles, and a readiness to have a frank group discussion or confidential side conversations, depending on the situation.

Trust is the glue that makes any team function at a high level, but it doesn't happen magically, especially in the case of a team composed of culturally diverse members. With the motivation to make things work and the tips above, you should be in a great position to leverage the benefits of diversity while minimizing its challenges.

———————

Andy Molinsky is a professor of organizational behavior and international management at Brandeis University and the author of *Global Dexterity* and *Reach*. His work helps people step outside their personal and cultural comfort zones. Download his free e-booklet of 10 powerful questions to help you step outside your comfort zone at andymolinsky.com/10powerfulquestions.

Ernest Gundling is a managing partner at Aperian Global, a firm that provides enterprise solutions to foster inclusive work environments, accelerate the development of future global leaders, and grow in new international markets. He is also a lecturer at the Haas School of Business, University of California, Berkeley, and the author of six books, including his most recent publication, *Inclusive Leadership, Global Impact.* Download a free chapter on inclusive leadership development at aperianglobal .com/resources/inclusive-leadership-global-impact/.

Build Resiliency and Support Mental Health

CHAPTER 22

Your Employees Want to Feel the Purpose in Their Jobs

by Dan Cable

No one wants to be a nine-to-five robot. People want to feel inspired, find meaning, and see the impact their work has on others. And when they do, they're more engaged, innovative, and productive. That isn't a secret or a revelation. It's common sense.

If you're a leader, helping others feel a sense of purpose can be a powerful tool. So, why then do so many leaders have trouble lighting up their employees?

Adapted from "Helping Your Team Feel the Purpose in Their Work," on hbr.org, October 22, 2019 (product #H058CA).

197

The simple answer is it's extremely difficult to instill purpose in others. It takes more than motivational talks, lofty speeches, or mission statements to spread purpose. In fact, if overblown or insincere, those methods can backfire, triggering cynical reactions.

Purpose is a grand word, but in the end, it's about helping people see their impact on others and helping them develop a story about why they love what they do. If you keep that in mind, and take a personal, authentic, and perpetual approach, you're likely to find success.

Make It Personal

First, purpose needs to be personal, and because purpose is meant to elicit an emotional reaction, purpose needs to be *felt*. You can't just talk about purpose.

Imagine you're the head of a college fundraising effort to help fund scholarships for underprivileged kids. How would you motivate your volunteers? According to a study by Adam Grant, if you stood in front of the group and talked about the impact of their work, you probably wouldn't improve anyone's performance. But if you invited a current scholarship recipient to share their personal story, that would be much more impactful. In fact, in Grant's study, after volunteers had listened to a scholarship recipient, they raised almost 400% more money than average.

When I was telling some leaders from F. Hoffmann-La Roche AG, one of the world's largest pharmaceutical companies, about the fundraising study, one of them blurted out, "This just happened to us!"

She explained how her team worked in the medical-devices division. Her group was sometimes looked down upon by people in the organization who thought that chemistry was "more sexy" than engineering. Many people in the division were not fully engaged, and the morale of the team was pretty low. One day the leader arranged for a customer to tell the team her personal story.

This customer had diabetes and had to test her blood daily to make sure her insulin dose was right. Unfortunately, this poor woman misunderstood how much blood was needed and was pricking her finger more than she needed to in order to get the blood. It not only hurt every day, so that it became something she dreaded, but she also was making a mess of her fingers. She would work her way down one finger from the tip to the knuckle, making it inflamed and sometimes infected, before moving to the next finger. She said it got to the point where she would sit on her hand to hide the damage from others. She stopped going out to dinner because she was so embarrassed.

The diabetic then told the group how they had improved her life when they invented a little finger-pricking device. You put it on the end of your finger and click it. It takes the absolute minimum amount of blood, is almost painless, and leaves almost no cut at all. She told how, because of this device, her hands have healed, and she can go out to dinner without feeling ashamed about herself. She told the group: "You people changed my life."

The Roche leader told us that the medical device team was really affected by this patient testimonial. She said that it was very emotional in the room during the meeting. And for months, people felt more purpose.

It doesn't matter what line of work you're in. If people see the cause and effect between their inputs and their team's progress, or understand the impact of a customer getting their product on time, or experience firsthand how their role is necessary to other people, they'll feel a sense of purpose.

Make It Authentic

But here's the thing. You need to believe what you're saying and doing. This makes all the difference. If your attempts at creating purpose do not align with your other leadership behaviors, employees will view your tactics as manipulative rather than inspirational.

Right after the woman at Roche shared her inspirational story, for example, a man on the other side of the room raised his hand and said, "Yeah, they tried that bullshit on us too."

"I have this boss who has never talked about anything but quarterly profits and hitting shipping targets," he continued. "Well, he must have come to London Business School and heard you talk about this study because one day he drags a patient into our weekly meeting and makes her tell us this story of how the drugs saved her life. I mean, trying to exploit our emotions to make us work harder? Using a patient to manipulate us?! That's pretty low."

We can learn so much through this exchange.

If you're a leader, and you're trying to sell people on purpose but you haven't acted consistently with that purpose in the past, your message will backfire. Humans are authenticity-detection machines: We're attracted to sincerity and repulsed by lies and insincerity.

So tread lightly. If you're personally inspired by listening to customers, and really believe in what you're saying, then go for it. If you're not, you might create more feelings of manipulation than inspiration.

Make It Perpetual

Even if you make purpose personal and authentic, you can't just do it once. Instead, you need to make it a routine.

Dr. Dorothee Ritz, the general manager of Microsoft in Austria, encourages her employees to go out in the field and experience the clients' problems firsthand. One small team spent a week out on the street with police officers, trying to understand when and where remote data could help them. Another team spent two days in a hospital to observe and understand what it would really mean to help it become paperless.

Ritz said these immersion experiences were enlightening for people. She said they came back illuminated, and it was clear to her that employees' personal experiences increased their sense of purpose, since they witnessed the *why* of their work. Ritz watched employees dive into their projects with more energy and enthusiasm after they had witnessed the clients' needs themselves.

So after a year of experimenting with this initiative, Ritz put something more secure in place. She selected a set of key customers (whom she calls partners) across industries ranging from car manufacturing to retailers to hospitals. And then 15 people from Microsoft—a team ranging from senior leaders to associates—went on-site at each company and asked lots of people at lots of different levels: "What are your challenges?" They talked to people in IT, of course, but they also talked with business decision makers across different functions.

At Tesla, for example, Ritz told me how Microsoft employees at different levels got to practice a conversation that started with Tesla's needs instead of Microsoft's products. They focused on holes in the process that Tesla needed to address. At a major retailer, a Microsoft employee who was very close to the Xbox asked some very grounded questions about issues with the console. This led to a useful, practical discussion rather than high-level executive speak, which helped move the whole conversation toward practical solutions that the team could go back and work on. These Microsoft teams came away with a few new contacts. But Ritz said what was even more important, these teams understood the purpose of the projects based on witnessing the situation and hearing about the companies' issues firsthand.

Ritz invested deeply in client experiences that allowed employees to witness the impact of their jobs firsthand, which helped them build emotional connections with the client and the work, and which helped Microsoft explore and learn as an organization.

Purpose can be a powerful tool for leaders who want to inspire people to bring their best to work. But most leaders agree that employees do not "get" their organizations' purpose. This is because purpose is personal and emotional. It is often managed poorly by transactional leaders who deliver speeches about lofty societal goals rather than helping put employees in direct contact with the people they serve. Purpose can work wonders for employee contributions when leaders start with a personal, authentic, and perpetual approach.

———————

Dan Cable is a professor of organizational behavior at London Business School. His newest book, *Exceptional*, helps you build a personal highlight reel to unlock your potential, and *Alive at Work* helps you understand the neuroscience of why people love what they do.

CHAPTER 23

Help Your Team Bounce Back from Failure

by Amy Gallo

No one likes to fail. And while we all know the importance of learning from mistakes, both individuals and teams can struggle to bounce back from big blunders. Whether it was a project that didn't meet its targets or an important deadline that you all missed, what can you do to help your employees recover? How can you help them see the experience as an opportunity for growth instead of the kiss of death?

Adapted from "How to Help Your Team Bounce Back from Failure," on hbr.org, February 27, 2015 (product #H01WMD).

What the Experts Say

It's often harder to lead a team past a failure than it is to help one person. "People are coming into projects with different expectations, perspectives, levels of investment, and different things at stake," explains Susan David, a founder of the Harvard/McLean Institute of Coaching and the author of the HBR article "Emotional Agility." "Some people may be very resilient, and others might feel more bruised," says Ben Dattner, an organizational psychologist and author of *The Blame Game.* "All the things that individuals fall prey to—misattribution and rationalization—are compounded on a team and add exponential complexity to the process." It doesn't matter whether one person on your team is at fault or if everyone bears some of the responsibility, it's your job as the manager to help the entire group move on. Here's how.

First, take control of your own emotions

Research shows that a leader's feelings are far more contagious than a team member's, so while "you don't want to suppress your emotions, you don't want to get stuck in a moody, negative space either," says David.[1] Do whatever you need to move on from the disappointment so that you're ready to help your team deal with theirs. And don't try to fake it. You need to be genuinely in control of your feelings or your team will see through you.

Give them space

At the same time, you shouldn't become a "beacon of positivity" before the team is ready, David says. It's OK to let everyone wallow in "disappointment and negative feelings" for a little while. She points to a client whose team lost a client pitch they'd been working on for months. It happened on a Friday and on Monday morning she came in saying, "Let's move on." Although she was trying to be motivating and forward-focused, to her devastated team, she "came off as uncaring and uncommitted." In fact, negative or neutral emotions are conducive to deductive reasoning, which means they can help your team more effectively process and analyze the failure. When you acknowledge the disappointment—with comments like "We're feeling down" or "This is tough for us"—"you're not just stroking people's emotions. You're facilitating a critical appraisal of the situation."

Be clear about what went wrong

Don't sugarcoat what happened or resort to "corporate speak" that abdicates responsibility. Avoid phrases like "Let's look on the bright side," "We're lucky it happened this way," "We suboptimized," or "A mistake was made." Instead, be clear: "We missed the deadline because we didn't take into account how long each task would take." When you focus on the facts, Dattner says, you can call it like it is without being demotivating.

But don't point fingers

"It's more important to focus on what's to blame, rather than who is to blame," Dattner says. If the fault really does lie with one person or a few people, then talk to those individuals in private and focus on their actions, not character. Dattner suggests you say something like:

"Here's the mistake you made. It doesn't mean that you're a bad person, but we need to understand why so it doesn't happen again and we can move on." You can also address the group, but be sure to do it in a way that doesn't single anyone out. David recommends an exercise where each team member writes down and shares a piece of feedback for each person on the team. "This allows for personal feedback that is also equitable," she explains.

Shift the mood

At some point, it's also important to move on from analyzing the failure to talking about what comes next. "The mutual commiserating and examination of what went wrong is useful only up to a point," says David. After a day or two (or maybe longer if the failure was a big one), push your team to more strategic, open-minded thinking and discuss how you will avoid similar mistakes in the future. Call a meeting and make sure that the tone is positive and energized. Dattner says you can use humor to lighten the mood.

Tell a story

You can help everyone begin to see the experience as a learning one by telling them about a mistake you've made in the past. "It can be very powerful when a leader authentically shares a time when they have a crucible-type failure that became a stepping-stone in their career," says David. If you don't have a story—or don't feel comfortable sharing it—consider drawing one or two out from the group. You could say something like: "We've all been on failed projects that ultimately proved to be constructive. Would anyone be willing to share?"

Encourage collaboration

Then have a conversation about the lessons learned from this experience. Don't lecture; discuss. David recommends dividing the team up into two groups: One half thinks through what could go wrong in future projects, while the other half focuses on the positive—what the team can change going forward. It's important to "focus more on solutions than problems, more on the future than the past," says Dattner.

Case Study: Allow your team to vent

Chris Bullock (not his real name) and his five-person team were responsible for upgrading application software for his company's most challenging client. This involved a large data migration, which did not go as planned. The day after the group turned the switch on the migration, they noticed that the system wasn't working properly and calls from the client started coming in. While Bullock and his team hadn't written the actual code, they had been the ones in charge when it failed, so many at the company were blaming them. They were disappointed and angry. "We put a lot of time and late nights into the project, and for it to fail—and so spectacularly—was embarrassing," he says.

The team worked through the weekend to fix the problem. On Monday, Bullock left them alone. "For me, these types of failures are like bereavements, and as such, people need to work through a similar process," he explains.

On Wednesday, the group met to talk about what had gone wrong. They discussed questions like: "Could we have spotted it sooner? Why hadn't the test cases found it?" This allowed them to vent their frustrations to each other. As a result, by Thursday, they were ready to have a much more constructive discussion with a larger group about how to do things differently next time around.

"We got back on the horse quickly and did the upgrade again two weeks later, and this time, with a successful result," Bullock says. The team learned a lot from the experience—most important that they were "stronger together."

Amy Gallo is a contributing editor at *Harvard Business Review* and the author of the *HBR Guide to Dealing with Conflict at Work* (Harvard Business Review Press, 2017) and the forthcoming *Getting Along: How to Work with Anyone (Even Difficult People)*. She writes and speaks about workplace dynamics. Follow her on Twitter @amyegallo.

NOTE

1. Thomas Sy and Stephane Cote, "The Contagious Leader: Impact of the Leader's Mood on the Mood of Group Members, Group Affective Tone, and Group Process," *Journal of Applied Psychology* 90, no. 2 (2005): 295–305.

CHAPTER 24

Managing an Employee Who's Having a Personal Crisis

by Carolyn O'Hara

We all have life events that distract us from work from time to time—an ailing family member, a divorce, the death of a friend. You can't expect someone to be at their best at such times. But as a manager, what *can* you expect? How can you support the person to take care of themselves emotionally while also making sure they are doing their work (or as much of it as they are able to)?

Adapted from "How to Manage an Employee Who's Having a Personal Crisis," on hbr.org, July 5, 2018 (product #H04FDO).

What the Experts Say

Managing an employee who is going through a stressful period is "one of the real challenges all bosses face," says Linda Hill, professor at Harvard Business School. Most of us try to keep work and home separate, but "we all have situations in which our personal and professional lives collide," and how you handle these situations with your employees is often a test of your leadership. You need to be empathetic and compassionate while also being professional and keeping your team productive. It's a fine line to maintain, says Annie McKee, a senior fellow at the University of Pennsylvania Graduate School of Education and the author of *How to Be Happy at Work*. Here's how to manage an employee going through a personal crisis.

Make yourself available

"People don't always feel comfortable telling their boss" that a parent is gravely ill or that they feel stressed out in the wake of a crumbling relationship, says McKee. They may be too overwhelmed, or embarrassed that it is causing them to be late repeatedly or to miss deadlines. Often a manager's first challenge is simply recognizing the warning signs that an employee is going through a difficulty. Invest time in building good relationships with employees so that you'll be able to detect any problems early on. If you maintain an atmosphere of compassion in the office, people are more likely to proactively come to you when they're going through a tough period.

Don't pry

As a leader, you need to be able to show empathy and care, but you also must avoid becoming an employee's personal confidante. After all, your job as manager is not to be the office shrink. So don't ask a bunch of questions about the employee's problems. As the person with less power in the relationship, the employee may feel compelled to tell you more than they're comfortable with. "You want to build a caring relationship with employees, not a friendly relationship," says Hill. Many managers make the mistake of confusing being liked with being trusted or respected. A good manager "has the ability to read and understand other people's needs and concerns," says McKee, while still keeping everyone focused on the major task at hand: accomplishing work.

Listen first, suggest second

When you speak to an employee about their current struggles, "listen first instead of immediately advocating for some particular course of action," says Hill. They may just want a sounding board about the difficulties of caring for a sick relative or an opportunity to explain why a divorce has affected their attention span. If you immediately suggest they take a leave of absence or adjust their schedule, they may be put off if that's not what they were thinking. Instead, ask what both of you can do together to address the issue of performance during the difficult period. "Try to use the word 'we,'" advises Hill, as in "How can *we* support *you*?" The employee may have an idea for a temporary arrangement—some time off, handing off a project to a colleague, or a more flexible schedule for a few weeks—that is amenable to you.

Know what you can offer

You may be more than willing to give a grieving employee several weeks of leave, or to offer a woman with a high-risk pregnancy the ability to work from home. But the decision isn't always yours to make. "You may be very compassionate but you may be in a company where that's not the way it works," says Hill. Of course, if you have the leeway to get creative with a flexible schedule, an adjusted workload, or a temporary work-from-home arrangement, do what you think is best. But also be sure you understand your company's restrictions on short- and long-term leave, and what, if any, bureaucratic hurdles exist before promising anything to your employee. Explain that you need to check what's possible before you both commit to an arrangement.

If the employee needs counseling or drug or alcohol services, there may be resources provided by your company's medical insurance that you can recommend. But investigate the quality of those resources first. "The last thing you want to do is send a suffering employee to avail themselves of a program or supposedly helpful people who then fall short," says McKee.

Check in regularly to make sure they're doing OK

Whether you've settled on a solution yet or not, check in with your employee occasionally by dropping by their desk (keeping their privacy in mind) or sending a brief email. Not only will your employee appreciate that you care, you'll get a better sense of how they are coping. "You can simply ask, 'Do you feel like you've got a handle on it?,'" says Hill. "And if they do, you can say, 'Let's just keep in touch so neither one of us has too many surprises. Or if you get a little over your head, I hope you'll feel free to come to me and we can do some more problem solving and make further adjustments if necessary.'"

Consider workload

You also have to consider whether prolonged absences will adversely affect clients or team members. If so, mitigate those risks by easing the person's workload. If there are people who are willing and able to take on some of the individual's projects, you can do that temporarily. Just be sure to reward the people who are stepping in. And then set timelines for any adjustments you make. If the person knows that their situation will last for six to eight weeks, set a deadline for you to meet and discuss what will happen next. Of course, many situations will be open-ended, and in those cases, you can set interim deadlines when you get together to check in on how things are going and make adjustments as necessary. Whatever arrangements you make, be crystal clear about your expectations during this time period. Be realistic about what they can accomplish and set goals they can meet. "For this to be useful," says McKee, "it's got to be specific and it has be grounded in reality."

Be transparent and consistent

Be conscious of the fact that other employees will take note of how you treat the struggling colleague and will likely expect similar consideration if they too run into difficult times in the future. "If you want to get productive work out of people, they need to trust you and believe that you'll treat them fairly," says Hill. Remember that policies may be precedent-setting. Every situation will be unique, but you want to be comfortable with policies in case you are called to apply them again. Keep in mind that solutions could apply to "the next person and the next and the next after that," says McKee.

Case Study: Set realistic goals and delegate some of the employee's work

Alicia Shankland, a senior HR executive with more than 20 years of experience, managed two different women through the intensely stressful, emotional months of fertility treatment. In both cases, the treatments continued for nearly a year, so the women were away from work frequently for medical appointments and procedures. They also experienced severe ups and downs from the hormone drugs and the emotional devastation of miscarriages.

What's more, the schedule of fertility treatments didn't fit neatly into any of the existing standard HR leave policies. "There was no way to make a 30-, 60-, 90-day plan to accommodate all the unknowns," Shankland said.

In each case, she endeavored to make as many allowances as possible, and the women used sick time, flex time, and personal days. She worked with each of them to set concrete, realistic work goals that allowed them to focus on the most critical deliverables while delegating other duties, and teammates pitched in to make sure duties weren't neglected or dropped. "We managed through it as a tight-knit team," she says.

A happy outcome was that the team was well prepared to cover for the maternity leaves that each woman eventually took. "It actually showed us all that we could play multiple roles," Shankland says. When the women returned from their respective maternity leaves, they were both at "110%." Each had "exceptionally successful years at the company that more than made up for the time when they needed extra hands to make it through."

Carolyn O'Hara is a writer and editor based in New York City. She has worked at the *Week*, *PBS NewsHour*, and *Foreign Policy*. Follow her on Twitter @carolynohara1.

CHAPTER 25

Reduce the Stigma of Mental Health at Work

by Diana O'Brien and Jen Fisher

Experts tell us that one in four adults will struggle with a mental health issue during their lifetime.[1] At work, those suffering—from clinical conditions or more minor ones—often hide it for fear that they may face discrimination from peers or even bosses. These stigmas can and must be overcome. But it takes more than policies set at the top. It also requires empathetic action from managers on the ground.

We count ourselves among those who have wrestled with mental health challenges. One morning a few years

Adapted from "5 Ways Bosses Can Reduce the Stigma of Mental Health at Work," on hbr.org, February 19, 2019 (product #H04SVU).

ago, in the midst of a successful year, Jen couldn't get out of bed. As a driven professional, she had ignored all the warning signs that she was experiencing post-traumatic stress disorder (PTSD). But her mentor, Diana, could see something was wrong, and when Jen couldn't come to work, the gravity of the situation became even clearer. In the ensuing weeks, we worked together to get Jen the help she needed.

Diana understood Jen's struggles because she had been there, too—not with PTSD but with anxiety. As the mother of adult triplets with autism and a busy professional, she'd often had difficulty managing things in her own life.

Throughout both of our careers, we have moved across the spectrum of mental health from thriving to barely hanging on, and somewhere in between. What we've learned through our own experiences is how much managerial support matters.

When bosses understand mental health issues—and how to respond to them—it can make all the difference for an employee professionally and personally. This involves taking notice, offering a helping hand, and saying, "I'm here, I have your back, you are not alone."

That's exactly what Jen said when a coworker told her that he was grappling with anxiety; it had gotten to the point where it was starting to impact his work and his relationships at home. He came to her because she'd been open about her own struggles. She listened to him, worked to understand what accommodations he needed, and told him about available resources, such as employee assistance programs. Then she continued to check in to see he was getting support he needed and make it clear that she and others were there to help.

How do you learn or teach the people on your team to address colleagues' or direct reports' mental health issues in the same way? Here are five ways managers can help drive a more empathetic culture.

Pay attention to language

We all need to be aware of the words we use that can contribute to stigmatizing mental health issues: "Mr. OCD is at it again—organizing everything." "She's totally schizo today!" "He is being so bipolar this week—one minute he's up, the next he's down." We've heard comments like these, maybe even made them ourselves. But through the ears of a colleague who has a mental health challenge, they can sound like indictments. Would you open up about a disorder or tell your team leader you needed time to see a therapist after hearing these words?

Rethink "sick days"

If you have cancer, no one says, "Let's just push through" or "Can you learn to deal with it?" They recognize that it's an illness and you'll need to take time off to treat it. If you have the flu, your manager will tell you to go home and rest. But few people in business would react to emotional outbursts or other signs of stress, anxiety, or manic behavior in the same way. We need to get more comfortable with the idea of suggesting and requesting days to focus on improving mental as well as physical health.

Encourage open and honest conversations

It's important to create safe spaces for people to talk about their own challenges, past and present, without fear of being called "unstable" or passed up for the next big project or promotion. Employees shouldn't fear that they will be judged or excluded if they open up in this way. Leaders can set the tone for this by sharing their own experiences, as we've done, or stories of other people who have struggled with mental health issues, gotten help, and resumed successful careers. They should also explicitly encourage everyone to speak up when feeling overwhelmed or in need.

Be proactive

Not all stress is bad, and people in high-pressure careers often grow accustomed to it or develop coping mechanisms. However, prolonged unmanageable stress can contribute to worsening symptoms of mental illness. How can managers ensure their employees are finding the right balance? By offering access to programs, resources, and education on stress management and resilience building. In our marketplace survey on employee burnout, nearly 70% of respondents said that their employers were not doing enough to prevent or alleviate burnout. Bosses need to do a better job of helping their employees connect to resources before stress leads to more serious problems.

Train people to notice and respond

Most offices keep a medical kit around in case someone needs a bandage or an aspirin. We've also begun to train our people in Mental Health First Aid, a national program proven to increase people's ability to recognize the signs of someone who may be struggling with a mental health challenge and connect them to support resources. Through role-plays and other activities, they offer guidance in how to listen nonjudgmentally, offer reassurance, and assess the risk of suicide or self-harm when, for example, a colleague is suffering a panic attack or reacting to a traumatic event. These can be difficult, emotionally charged conversations, and they can come at unexpected times, so it's important to be ready for them.

When your people are struggling, you want them to be able to open up and ask for help. These five strategies can help any boss or organization create a culture that ceases to stigmatize mental illness.

Diana O'Brien retired from her role as global chief marketing officer of Deloitte and is currently a board member and business adviser.

Jen Fisher is Deloitte's chief well-being officer in the United States.

NOTE

1. "Mental Health by the Numbers," National Alliance on Mental Illness, March 2021, https://www.nami.org/Learn-More/Mental -Health-By-the-Numbers.

CHAPTER 26

Make Work Less Stressful and More Engaging

by Natalia Peart

We all know that excessive stress is a health hazard. What is less talked about are the effects of burnout on business performance. Stress makes people nearly three times as likely to leave their jobs, temporarily impairs strategic thinking, and dulls creative abilities.[1] Burnout, then, is a threat to your bottom line, one that costs the United States more than $300 billion a year in absenteeism,

---

Adapted from "Making Work Less Stressful and More Engaging for Your Employees," on hbr.org, November 5, 2019 (product #H058FR).

turnover, diminished productivity, and medical, legal, and insurance costs.[2]

The more companies realize this, the more the workplace wellness sector grows. But individual-level perks like on-site gyms and nap rooms are not the answer to our problem. In a 2019 study, researchers Zirui Song and Katherine Baicker found that while there is an expectation that wellness programs will reduce healthcare spending and absenteeism within a year or two, they often do not. This study adds to the growing body of work suggesting that such programs are not as effective as we think.

Instead, employers need to shift to organization-level approaches for reducing stress at work, ones that foster employee well-being while simultaneously improving business performance. While this may seem unrealistic, it's not. Over a decade of experience as a clinical psychologist and leadership consultant has taught me that burnout prevention requires reducing workplace stress while also upping employee engagement. Here's how to do both.

Create a Work Environment That Decreases Stress

When employees are put in a high-stress situation—whether from unclear expectations, unreasonable deadlines, or a hectic workspace—they are at risk of moving into fight-or-flight mode. This is something that happens to our bodies when we feel threatened. The primal, more emotional parts of our brains take over, and our ability to think long term, strategize, and innovate decreases. If we stay in this mode too long, eventually we get burned out. To counter this effect, you need to build a secure work environment and incorporate stress reduction habits into your team's daily workflows.

Increase psychological safety

If your employees perceive your workplace as a threat, then you cannot build the trust your team needs to collaborate and innovate effectively. In her book, *The Fearless Organization*, Amy Edmondson describes three steps you can take to build psychological safety. First, make your expectations obvious by giving your employees clear goals. Second, make sure everyone feels that their voices are heard, and that everyone knows you *want* their voices to be heard. You can do this by inviting people to speak up in meetings and conducting brainstorming sessions more than you impose top-down decisions. Third, develop a work environment that is both challenging and unthreatening. Let people know it's OK to fail. Recognize team members who think outside the box, and ask your employees for feedback regularly to show you're all in it together. (For more on psychological safety, see chapter 6.)

Build regular break times into the workday

The human brain can focus for around 90–120 minutes before it needs to rest.[3] That's why you should encourage your employees to step away from their desks and mentally disengage from challenging tasks every couple of hours. Suggest they go for a short walk (especially if they have been in a series of long meetings), send out calendar invites reminding them to take breaks, and try to lead by example. Letting their minds rest and moving their bodies will provide your team with the mental space they need to perform well consistently.

Encourage the use of private workspaces when team members need to focus

Open offices are prone to distractions, increasing stress and decreasing productivity. There is sometimes a built-in expectation that employees must always be available for impromptu meetings and discussions as a result of the office layout. If you don't have private workspaces where employees can go to focus or decompress, try using signals like "do not disturb" signs when needed or scheduling "quiet hours" when people can work.

Set boundaries around time outside of work

Teams that are not all in one location might need to work outside of traditional hours from time to time. However, the blurring of work and personal time is a significant source of job stress. A 2018 study by William J. Becker and two colleagues found that it is not just answering emails that increases employees' anxiety—it is also the expectation that they will be available to do so outside of work hours. To combat this, set clear guidelines and follow them. Send emails and make calls after hours only when it's urgent—and set the bar very high.

Look into flexible work policies

If you want a highly adaptive team, then create an adaptable work environment. Give your employees flexibility by allowing them to work staggered hours, taking into account their varying needs. Hold one-on-one meetings to understand those needs and find alternative arrangements for people who are struggling with work-life balance.

Build Employee Engagement

Decades of data have confirmed that higher employee engagement, or the strength of the mental and emotional connection an employee feels toward their workplace, has many positive benefits—including reduced stress and improved health, job satisfaction, productivity, retention, and profitability.

Be transparent

If your team members are confused about how their work connects to and serves both the short- and long-term company goals, they will naturally become more stressed and less productive, especially in times of uncertainty. Part of your job is to help them see the big picture, or the role they play in helping the company achieve its larger goals. While you may not be able to share everything with your team, you can provide them with the information they need to understand how their work is contributing to the company's mission. If they are curious about something that you are unable to share, be transparent about why. You want to reduce the stress that accompanies ambiguity. A Gallup study of 2.5 million teams found that, when managers communicated daily with their direct reports, employees were three times as likely to be engaged as when their managers did not communicate regularly with them. Still, only 40% of employees say they are well informed about their company's strategic goals.[4]

Make sure people are in the right roles

If your team members loathe doing their jobs, then they are naturally going to be less engaged. To ensure that their talents and strengths are aligned with the expectations and responsibilities of their roles, check in with each of your direct reports regularly. These conversations don't need to be formal—talk to them about their passions, interests, and goals. Use the information you gather to assign projects they will find meaningful, and follow up to ensure they have the tools they need to succeed.

Give as much autonomy as you can

When possible, give your team control over how they manage their projects. Employees are 43% less likely to experience high levels of burnout when they have a choice in deciding what tasks to do, when to do them, and how much time to spend on each.[5] To make sure someone is ready to work independently, one researcher suggests asking them to shadow you on a task or project first, and then allowing them to practice under your supervision. During this time, you can give them feedback and gauge when they will be ready to work on their own.

Demonstrate a commitment to your employees' growth and progression

Don't hold on too tightly to your talent. While most people will not be promoted every year or two, they do need to feel that you are providing them with steady growth and learning opportunities. Sometimes this might even mean supporting internal mobility. Give people the chance to move around, or move on, if it's the right next step for their careers. Your commitment to their growth will deepen the sense of trust between you and them.

Create a culture of recognition

Publicly recognizing the hard work and contributions of team members decreases feelings of stress and increases feelings of connection and belonging. Research has shown that companies with high-recognition cultures perform better and have less turnover than those that don't. This is, perhaps, because support and recognition make it easier for people to cope with the demands of work by showing them that their efforts are valued. Team meetings are a great time to call out exceptional performance. Unexpected gestures that communicate sincere appreciation can also be effective. If your employee closes a new client deal, for example, congratulate them publicly. Deloitte's research on engagement shows that if you can create a culture in which peers recognize and show gratitude to one another, your employees are more likely to stay happy and satisfied in their roles.

Deepen engagement further by instilling a sense of purpose

If the only thing motivating your team to go to work is a paycheck, their performance will suffer more than those who feel a sense of purpose in what they do. When employees connect the impact of their work back to the real world, daily tasks that once seemed tedious gain meaning. Start by making purpose a part of your business plan. Even if it's not declared in your mission statement, help your team understand by showing them the impact their work has within the company, in other departments, outside the organization, and even on society. You should also share your purpose during recruitment, and search for candidates who support it.

Burnout and the consequences it reaps when unacknowledged are detrimental to employee well-being and business performance. To battle this growing epidemic and create healthier work environments, leaders need to commit to changing what "workplace wellness" looks like. Let these steps guide you. If you are successful, you will not just reduce worker stress. You will create a workforce with happier, more productive employees, and the business will be better for it.

Natalia Peart is a clinical psychologist and *Fortune* 1000 executive leadership consultant. She has served on the Federal Reserve Board, 10th District, as staff psychologist at Johns Hopkins, and as CEO of the Women's Center for Advancement. She is also the author of *Future Proofed: The New Rules of Success in Work & Life for Our Modern World*.

NOTES

1. Ben Wigert and Sangeeta Agrawal, "Employee Burnout, Part 1: The 5 Main Causes," Gallup, July 12, 2018, https://www.gallup.com/workplace/237059/employee-burnout-part-main-causes.aspx.

2. "Workplace Stress," American Institute of Stress, https://www.stress.org/workplace-stress.

3. Tony Schwartz, "For Real Productivity, Less Is Truly More," hbr.org, May 17, 2010, https://hbr.org/2010/05/for-real-productivity-less-is.

4. Paul J. Zak, "The Neuroscience of Trust," *Harvard Business Review*, January–February 2017.

5. Ryan Pendell, "Millennials Are Burning Out, Gallup, July 19, 2018, https://www.gallup.com/workplace/237377/millennials-burning.aspx.

Index

Notes

Notes